A Little Book of Robin Hood

The Five Early Ballads

A Little Book of Robin Hood

The Five Early Ballads

Michael Dacre

Series Originator: Fiona Collins

First published 2013

The History Press
The Mill, Brimscombe Port
Stroud, Gloucestershire, GL5 2QG
www.thehistorypress.co.uk

British Library Cataloguing in Publication Data.
A catalogue record for this book is available from the British Library.

ISBN 978 0 7524 8967 4

Typesetting and origination by The History Press
Printed in Great Britain
Manufacturing managed by Jellyfish Solutions Ltd

Ancient Legends Retold: An Introduction to the Series

This book represents a new and exciting collaboration between publishers and storytellers. It is part of a series in which each book contains an ancient legend, reworked for the page by a storyteller who has lived with and told the story for a long time.

Storytelling is the art of sharing spoken versions of traditional tales. Today's storytellers are the carriers of a rich oral culture, which is flourishing across Britain in storytelling clubs, theatres, cafés, bars and meeting places, both indoors and out. These storytellers, members of the storytelling revival, draw on books of traditional tales for much of their repertoire.

The partnership between The History Press and professional storytellers is introducing a new and important dimension to the storytelling revival. Some of the best contemporary storytellers are creating definitive versions of the tales they love for this series. In this way, stories first found on the page, but shaped 'on the wind' of a storyteller's breath, are once more appearing in written form, imbued with new life and energy.

My thanks go first to Nicola Guy, a commissioning editor at The History Press, who has championed the series, and secondly to my friends and fellow storytellers, who have dared to be part of something new.

Fiona Collins, Series Originator, 2013

Introduction

In this little book you will find the best of Robin Hood. The five earliest ballads are the cream of the jest. They are violent, earthy, vigorous, passionate, mysterious, funny, frightening and, ultimately, tragic, as a national epic should be. Robin Hood complements King Arthur. As King Arthur is meet entertainment for the nobility, so the merry tales of Robin Hood are meat and drink for the common folk. In these five early ballads, and one later play, Robin is himself a commoner, a yeoman, a working-class hero, not the ousted, disaffected Saxon earl into which the later ballads try to turn him, probably to please a Norman nobility that was beginning to enjoy him in spite of itself.

Here we have the essential Robin Hood, the real Robin Hood, stripped of the romanticism that would clothe him in noble weeds or the mysticism that would seek to make of him some New Age spirit of the forest, related to Herne the Hunter or Robin Goodfellow. Here you will find a Robin Hood of fast action, hot temper and unswerving hatred toward the powers that be, especially the power of the Church and the highly paid flunkies, such as the Sheriff of Nottingham.

Was there a real Robin Hood? It is probable that we shall never know. Most of the early collectors of these ballads assumed that Robin Hood was the invention of the ballad-makers, that the mediaeval ballad-mongers created Robin Hood to appease a disaffected peasantry, still largely Saxon, that continued to suffer under an intolerable Norman oppression. However, research carried out in the nineteenth century by a man who had access to mediaeval records points to a possibility for an historical Robin Hood.

In 1838 Joseph Hunter became the assistant keeper of the new Public Record Office and worked on the editing and publishing of mediaeval government records. The son of a Sheffield cutler and a professional antiquarian from South Yorkshire, Hunter could not well ignore the question of Robin Hood's identity. In *The Geste of Robyn Hode*, the king is identified as 'Edward our comely king' three times. Between April and November 1323, Edward II made a royal progress through Yorkshire and Lancashire, ending up at Nottingham. In 1317 a Robert Hood and his wife Matilda appeared in the court rolls of the manor of Wakefield, which is only ten miles from Barnsdale, the scene of Robin Hood's exploits in the early ballads; while between 24 March and 22 November 1324, a Robyn Hode was recorded as being in the royal service as one of the porters of the chamber. The names Robert and Robin were interchangeable at that time. This does seem convincing and corroborates the events described in the *Geste*.

However, J.C. Holt, in his book *Robin Hood* (considered by many to be the definitive work on the subject), points out that the Robert Hood of Wakefield is not necessarily the Robyn Hode who was later in the king's service; that there is no evidence that the Wakefield Robert Hood was ever an outlaw; and that on 27 June 1323 Robyn Hode received his wages, according to a day-book of the chamber (only recently made legible by ultraviolet light), confirming that he was already in the king's service before Edward II came to Nottingham. Even so, I am not entirely convinced by Mr Holt's arguments.

It is feasible that Robyn entered King Edward's service earlier in the year, on his way north. It is conceivable that Robert Hood of Wakefield was forced into outlawry because he supported the Earl of Lancaster's rebellion against Edward (the Earl was executed following his defeat at the Battle of Boroughbridge in 1322) and that the outlaws were all disaffected soldiers who had been on the losing side. That there is no mention of him after 1317 does not necessarily mean that he had died: it might simply mean that he had been outlawed and had gone into hiding in Barnsdale. The final reference to Robyn Hode, porter of the king's chamber, appears in the day-book for 22 November 1324, when he was paid off: 'To Robyn Hod, formerly one of the porters, because he can no longer work, five shillings as a gift, by command.' Holt maintains that 'This was not the Robin Hood of the *Geste* who left the court through boredom to return to the greenwood where he lived for twenty-two years before his fatal journey to Kirklees', as 'because he can no longer work' suggests old age.

But I have often found, as a storyteller, that the story can be trusted – that is to say, that the old tales often contain more truth than the historians credit them – and the *Geste* says that Robin Hood's king was Edward, and that Robyn 'dwelled in the kynges courte But twelve monethes and thre'. On 27 June 1323, Robyn Hode received his wages; and on 22 November 1324, Robyn Hod was paid off with 5 shillings. That is a period of eighteen months in which a Robyn Hode served King Edward II as a porter of his chamber. So the author of the *Lytell Geste* got the timing slightly wrong and forgot to say that Robyn entered the king's service during his progress north, before he got to Nottingham. This is no more than dramatic licence. The names speak for themselves.

A Geste of Robyn Hode is quite clear about Robin's reasons for leaving King Edward's employment. He has spent £100 and all his men's 'fee' on payments to knights and squires 'To gete hym grete renowne' and all his men have deserted him, except for Little John and Will Scathelocke. He sees some young men shooting and cries out, 'Alas! My welthe is went away.' And later, 'Alas and well a way. Yf I dwele lenger with the kynge, Sorowe wyll me slay.' It is all too obvious from this that Robin Hood is heartily sick of the life at court – the bribes, the privilege, the endless spending of money to maintain a place in the pecking order – and that he longs for the clean air of the greenwood.

Edward II's court was infamous for its decadence and instability, and it may well have been Robin's intention to get out while the going was good, for the barons were furious about the king's relationship with his favourites, Piers Gaveston and Hugh Despenser. Gaveston was murdered in 1312, while Despenser was brutally executed in 1326. Edward II himself did not have much longer to live. He was deposed by his wife and Roger Mortimer in 1326, and murdered in Berkeley Castle in 1327. Moreover, Robin Hood, as a simple yeoman and a notorious outlaw, would not have been held in high esteem by the powerful men at court. The greenwood would have been the safest place for him. But I write this as a storyteller, not as a historian, and I have to confess that the Edward II 'Robyn Hode' appeals to me as a good story rather than as a plausible historical theory. All the respected writers on Robin Hood, including R.B. Dobson and J. Taylor in *Rymes of Robyn Hood*, agree with J.C. Holt.

So I must confess to nurturing still a sneaking regard for the Robyn Hode who was most definitely in King Edward II's employ from 27 June 1323 until 24 November 1324. The name Robert or Robin Hood was like John Smith in the Middle Ages. There were hundreds of them, and perhaps that was the point. Robin Hood was an Everyman, who appealed to every man and woman who hated tyranny and loved a good story about the ordinary yeoman who got one over on the rich and their oppressive authorities. Why, Edward II, 'our cumlie kynge', handsome and effeminate as he may have been, was himself cruelly done to death by those very authorities. Perhaps he even paid off his favourite porter to get him out of the way, so that Robyn Hode at least would not fall foul of the unforgiving English barons and Edward's even more unforgiving wife, Isabella.

However, Sir James Holt points out that fyttes 7 and 8 of the *Geste* could have been written after Edward's circuit of the north, to give the legend a contemporary flavour; and we must concede the numerous mentions of 'Robynhode' names as far back as 1261, which seriously implies a thirteenth-century Robin Hood. Contemporary scholarship is unanimously in favour of this position, I am bound to admit, and the increase of 'Robynhod' surnames and nicknames from the mid-thirteenth century onward certainly points to the already established popularity of Robin Hood the outlaw from the time of Richard the Lionheart and Bad King John. In fact, this multiplication of 'Robyn Hodes' may imply that there was more than one of them.

There is one other possible candidate. On 25 July 1225, royal justices held assizes at York. Penalties included 32s 6d for the chattels of Robert Hod, fugitive. The account recurred in the following year and it means that Robert Hood had fled the jurisdiction of the court and was now a fugitive. He was an outlaw, and according to J.C. Holt 'the only possible original of Robin Hood, so far discovered, who is known to have been an outlaw'. This theory also places Robin Hood near the time of King John, when he is most popularly supposed to have operated.

And so Robyn Hode, one of the porters of the royal chamber, went back into the forest of Barnsdale, where he passes out of history and enters into legend; and twenty-two years later he was:

Begyled, I wys,
Through a wycked woman,
The pryoresse of Kyrkesly,
That nye was of his kynne,

For the love of a knyght,
Syr Roger of Donkester,
That was her owne speciall [sin?]:
Full evyll mote they fare!

They toke togyder theyr counsell
Robyn Hode for to sle,
And how they myght best do that dede,
His banis [bane] for to be.

Sir Roger of Donkestere,
By the Pryoresse he lay,
And there they betrayed good Robyn Hode,
Through theyr false play.

Cryst have mercy on his soule,
That dyed on the rode!
For he was a good outlawe,
And dyde pore men moch god.

Michael Dacre, 2013

One

Robin Hood and the Monk

In somer, when the shawes be sheyne,
And leves be large and long,
Hit is full mery in fayre foreste
To here the foulys song;

To se the dere draw to the dale
And leve the hilles hee
And shadow hem in the leves grene
Under the grene-wode tre.

It befell one Whitsuntide, early on a May morning, when the sun was up and shining and the birds were singing merrily, that Little John turned to Robin Hood as they stood at the edge of a forest glade.

'Oh, what a beautiful morning!' sang Little John. 'By Him that died on tree, there is no happier man than I in the whole of Christendom!' But Robin Hood was in a terrible mood and made no answer.

'Buck up, Master!' cried Little John. 'Open your eyes to the beauty of this May morning!'

'Aye, may be,' growled Robin, 'but one thing grieves my heart – that I may not go openly to Mass nor matins. It's more than a fortnight since I went to church to seek my Saviour. Well, to hell with it! Today I'm going into Nottingham, to hear Mass in St Mary's Church, and may the might of Mild Mary go with me!'

'If I was you,' said Much the Miller's Son, 'I'd take twelve strong men with you as well as the might of Mild Mary. I mean, anyone might have a go at you on your own, but there's not many would take on twelve.'

'By my faith!' cried Robin, 'I go to worship, not to war. Of all my Merry Men, I will take none but Little John here, and he can carry my bow.'

'You can carry your own bow,' said Little John, 'and I, Master, will carry mine. But look, we'd better have some practice before we go. Let's shoot for a penny under the trees here.'

'Shoot for a penny?' cried Robin Hood. 'With the greatest archer in England? I tell you, Little John, for every penny you put down, I'll hold up three.'

They started shooting at a stand of saplings on the other side of the glade and, such was Robin's mood that morning, he couldn't shoot for toffee and Little John won 5 shillings from him. Then a strange quarrel fell between them as they went upon their way, Little John insisting he'd won the 5 shillings and Robin Hood simply saying 'No!', until Little John grasped him by the shoulder and roared, 'Give me my

5 bob, you flipping little footpad!', whereupon Robin Hood turned on Little John and, jumping up as high as he could, punched the big man in the mouth. Little John got quite cross and pulled out his sword.

'If I didn't love you,' he said, 'I'd hit you – very hard. As it is, you can get some other fool to be your serf.' And he strode back into Sherwood Forest on paths well known to him, while Robin Hood went on into Nottingham alone.

As he slipped in through the gates, he prayed to Mary the Mother of God to bring him safely out again, as well he might, for such was his mood that morning that he refused to wear a disguise; so, when he entered St Mary's Church and knelt before the cross, everyone saw that it was Robin Hood, with his hair and beard of bright red curls, his hood and hose of Lincoln green, and his bow and arrows upon his back. Behind him stood a burly monk with a big head and a black habit and he knew Robin at once; so, as soon as he could, the monk sidled off through a side door and ran, as fast as his well-fed bulk would allow, to the Sheriff.

'Bar the gates!' he cried. 'That false outlaw, Robin Hood, is kneeling at Mass in St Mary's Church. Rise up, Sheriff, and take him! He robbed me once of £800 and I can never forget it!'

'Huh! He's done worse things to me I'll never forget!' growled the sheriff, and he rose and gave his orders to bar all the gates to the city. Then he armed himself and made off to the church, with many a mother's son, well-armed and white-faced, rattling along beside him through the dusty, crowded streets.

In at the church doors they thronged, swords in hand, baying for the blood of Robin Hood, heedless of the sanctity of the church and the screaming of the women and children.

'Oh dear,' said Robin to an old woman kneeling next to him, 'I'm beginning to miss Little John.'

But he drew out his great two-handed sword, for he would not use his bow in the crowded church, and ran straight to where the Sheriff and his men stood thickest. Three times he ran through them, swinging the huge sword like a madman, and many a mother's son was horribly mutilated that day and twelve of them died screaming of their wounds, but then his sword broke in two against the stronger steel of the sheriff's helmet.

'God curse the smith that made you!' gasped Robin, 'for now I'm weaponless, and unless I can get away from these bastards, they'll kill me, sure as shit!' Robin then ran through them out of the church, straight into the arms of the burly monk, who held him fast until the soldiers closed upon him and, because they wanted him alive, they beat him bloody and senseless and threw him into a dark and narrow dungeon deep beneath Nottingham Castle.

The sheriff received the big-headed monk in the public courtroom and thanked him drily for being the means of the outlaw's capture.

'Now go,' he said, 'and bring this good news to the king in London, for he alone can decide what to do with Robin Hood.' The sheriff offered the monk an escort of soldiers but the monk refused, thinking to get all the glory for himself, saying, 'No, no, I'll go alone, with but my little page for company and so we shall escape notice.'

But Robin Hood had many friends in the town and word spread like a forest fire that the black monk had betrayed the outlaw and was now on his way to the king; so, faster than the wind, a messenger sped to Sherwood and brought the news to the Merry Men. Then they were not quite so merry. Some of them wept and wailed and some just sat and stared, but all at once Little John was standing among them.

'Let up your meeping!' cried Little John. 'For God's sake, you're a gang of outlaws, not a flock of nellies! Robin's been in far worse scrapes before and got away with it. He's served Our Lady many a day and I trust her not to let him die a wicked death. So stop your puling!

I shall take this monk in hand, by the might of Mild Mary. No! Just me and Much will go. The rest of you stay here by the trysting-tree and prepare a feast for our return.'

Then away ran Much and Little John through the forest, bounding like deer through the sun-dappled glades, careering headlong down leafy dells, clearing streams at a single leap, panting up the steep slopes, until they came to an old ruined house that overlooked the London road. This had been Much's uncle's house and here they hid, Little John keeping watch at a broken window in an upper room; and soon they heard a clattering of hooves and here came the monk riding over the hill, his great black habit billowing in the wind, his little page riding behind.

'That's the one,' said Little John. 'I know him by his wide black hood. It's a shame about the boy, though.'

The two yeomen stepped out onto the highway, humbly and courteously, addressing the monk in friendly tones.

'Beg pardon, good father,' said Little John, 'but have you any news of that flipping little footpad, Robin Hood? He robbed me of 5 shillings only this morning but I hear the bastard's been taken, thank God.'

'Ha-ha, he robbed me too,' said the monk, reining in his horse, 'of £800 and more, but it was I that laid hands upon him, so you may thank me for it.'

'I pray God thank you,' said Little John, 'and we will when we may. But by your leave, we'll go with you a while, for Robin Hood leads many a wild fellow in these parts and if they knew you were riding here, they'd slaughter you like sheep.' And, as they went on their way, the monk and Little John talking and laughing together, John held on to the horse's reins, while Much watched the page, lest he should escape.

All of a sudden John reached up and caught hold of the monk's hood and pulled him off his horse, heedless that the wretch fell on his head. For Little John was in a terrible mood and he wrenched out his sword and raised it high above his head and the monk saw that he would soon be dead and he cried and wept for mercy in a shrill high voice.

'He was my master,' said Little John, 'that you have brought to grief, but never shall you tell your tales unto the king.' And Little John delayed no longer but sliced off the monk's head with one great blow, and Much pulled the little page down and cut off his head too, for fear that he would tell. They buried them both right there, 'twixt bog and heath, and then they rode to London with the Sheriff's letter. That got them into the king's presence, where Little John went down on one knee, crying boldly, 'God save you, my liege!' and gave the letter into the king's own hand.

The king unfolded it and read it and said, 'So might I thrive, there is no man in England I longed more to see than you. But where is the monk that should have brought this letter?'

'Ah!' said John, 'He was killed on the way in an ambush by Robin Hood's men. Only us two got away alive. But his death was worthy of him, I'll swear to that!'

'Indeed. Yes, well,' said the king. 'We'll have him buried with full honours in Westminster Abbey.' The king gave Much and Little John £20 apiece, made them Yeomen of the Crown with uniforms to match, and bade them go straight back to the sheriff with sealed orders to bring Robin Hood alive to appear before the king himself, and he ordained that no man should hinder them. They took their leave of the king and, on fresh mounts, without stopping, rode hell-for-leather back to Nottingham, where they found all the gates locked.

John called up to the porter, 'Why are all the gates locked?'

'Because Robin Hood is here in prison!' called down the porter, 'and his outlaws attack us every day, shooting at our men upon the walls!'

'Silly buggers,' muttered Little John, then called up, 'So let us in, you ninny! Don't you recognise the king's livery? We bear sealed orders from the king himself concerning Robin Hood!'

The porter hastily let them in and it wasn't long before they were standing face to face with the Sheriff of Nottingham, who doffed his hood as he broke the king's seal and read the letter.

'Where is the monk that bore my letter?' he said suddenly.

'Ah!' said John, 'the king is so fond of him, he's given him a place in Westminster Abbey.' That seemed to satisfy the sheriff and he gave them both a slap-up meal, with the best wine and ale, during which he said, 'We'll take him to London tomorrow with 300 men-at-arms.'

That night, in their quarters, John said to Much, 'We can't hope to rescue him tomorrow. We'll have to do it tonight.' And as soon as the sheriff was fast asleep, dead drunk as usual on his own wine and ale, the two outlaws made their way openly down into the dungeons. The soldiers on guard recognised the livery of the king and let them through, until they came to Robin's cell.

'Gaoler!' whispered Little John. 'We have secret orders from the king to slit Robin Hood's throat before he escapes from your incompetent sheriff. You can watch if you like. It'd be something to tell your grandchildren.' But as soon as the gaoler opened the outer door, Little John was upon him and had him pinned to the door by a knife through his throat and he never saw his grandchildren again. John took his keys and opened the inner door and stooped into the narrow, foul-smelling cell, where they found Robin chained to the wall, lying in his own filth and mouldy straw. Little John unchained him and great was their joy at seeing each other, though Robin could hardly stand. John and Much cleaned him up as best they could, dressed him in the gaoler's clothes and helped him back up the stairs, the hood pulled low over his face, back through all the soldiers, Little John grunting, 'Change of gaolers! This one drinks too much, just like the sheriff!'

The soldiers roared with laughter and the three outlaws made their way onto the battlements and there, where the wall was lowest, they let themselves down by a good strong rope that Much had found in the dungeons; and so they slipped away like shadows in the misty, pre-dawn light, back into the greenwood.

So it was that when the cock began to crow and the day began to break, the sheriff's men found the gaoler dead and Robin Hood gone. Oooh, the sheriff was upset. He wept and wailed and tore out his hair and ground his teeth to splinters.

'I will never dare come before the king again!' he cried, 'for if I do, he will surely hang me!' But when word came to Edward, our comely king, he said, in high anger, 'Little John has fooled the sheriff but in faith, he fooled me too, or else I should have hanged the sheriff. Sweet Jesu! I made them Yeomen of the Crown and gave them £20 each with my own hand. Truly, there is no yeoman like Little John in the whole of England. He is true to his master and he loves Robin Hood better than any of us. Robin is bound to him forever but let us speak no more of this, for Little John has fooled us all.'

And Robin Hood was in merry Sherwood, as light as leaf on tree, and Little John turned to him and said, 'The king has paid me the money you owed me, with interest, God save him. And I have paid you a good turn for an evil one and brought you safe back under the greenwood tree. You may pay me when you will. Now farewell and have a good day.'

'Nay, by my truth!' cried Robin Hood. 'So shall this never be! I make you the master, Little John, of all my men and me!'

'Nay, by my truth!' cried Little John. 'So shall that never be! Your good fellow and your friend – no other shall I be!' Then they embraced and kissed and wept on each other's shoulders and made merry under the fine-spun leaves, feasting on venison pasties, wine and ale, and they were glad.

Thus endys the talkying of the munke
And Robyn Hode i-wysse;
And God, that is ever oure on trew kyng
Bryng us all to His blisse!

Two

Robyn Hode and the Pottere

In schomer when the leves spryng,
The bloschoms on every bowe,
So merey doyt the berdys syng
Yn wodys merey nowe.

Hearken to me, good yeopersons,
Comely, courteous and good –
One of the best that ever bare bow,
His name was Robin Hood.

For Robin Hood was a simple peasant like us, a Saxon yeoman; he was never tainted with aristocratic blood, but for the love he bore to Our Lady, he worshipped all women, as you shall see.

One fine summer's morning, as he stood with Little John at the edge of Sherwood Forest, he saw a sturdy potter driving his cart over the meadow towards Nottingham.

'There's that by'r Lady potter again,' said Robin. 'He always comes this way, but he's never paid us a penny's road-tax in his life.'

'I'd like to see anyone make him,' said Little John. 'I met him once at Wentbridge Fair and he gave me a stroke with his staff as damn near stove my ribs in.'

'I'll bet you forty shillings,' said Robin, 'that I'll make this potter pay a toll.'

'You're on!' said Little John. Robin leaped out of the trees in front of the potter, crying, 'Stop!'

'What do you want, scum?' said the potter in a Brummy accent you could clean toilets with.

'Mr Scum to you,' said Robin, 'and I want a penny's road-tax.'

'And who the hell are you to demand road-tax?'

'My name is Robin Hood and you're paying me a toll for driving past my forest.'

'And my name's Rumpelstiltskin,' said the potter, 'and if you don't get out the way I'll put your head inside your bottom.' The potter jumped down, wielding a stout two-handed quarterstaff. Robin was armed with sword and shield – he wasn't taking any chances – and hard they went at it, these two good honest yeomen. But all at once, the potter swung a vicious backhand stroke that wrenched Robin's shield out of his grip, and then a reverse stroke that clubbed Robin in the neck and down he went. Little John ran to where his master lay groaning on the ground.

'Please don't put his head inside his bottom,' said Little John. 'He's all right, really – just a bit hot-tempered – it's the red hair, you see.'

'Well,' said the potter, 'if you ask me, it's bad manners to stop a working-class chap from doing his business.'

'By the grace of Mild Mary, you're right,' said Robin, struggling to his feet, 'and from now on, you can drive this way for free. What's your name, good potter, and will you be my friend?'

'My name is Much,' said the potter, 'and I'm the son of a miller – but look here, if you really are Robin Hood, can I be in your gang? Potting's all very well, but these Norman taxes are crippling me. Any road, I think I'm more suited to the life of an outlaw. I quite like fighting and knocking people down.'

'Much the Miller's Son!' cried Robin. 'You're in! And now, my Much of a Muchness, give me your clothes and I'll give you mine, for I've a mind to sell your pots in Nottingham.'

'All right,' said Much, 'but you must sell all my pots and get a good price for them and then I'll be free of them. Here, he is a bit queer, isn't he?' he said to Little John as he took his clothes off.

'Er – Master,' said Little John, 'you will look out for the Sheriff of Nottingham, won't you?'

'Mind your own business, John,' said Robin. 'The sheriff's wife will love these pots and she'll pay well for them, by Our Lady.' And when Robin and the potter had exchanged clothes, Robin shaved off all his red hair and beard, and rubbed his face and hands with potter's clay until even Little John didn't recognise him; then he drove the potter's cart off toward Nottingham while Much the Miller's Son walked back to the outlaw's camp with Little John, discussing Robin Hood's peculiar recruiting technique as they went.

When Robin drove into Nottingham, he stabled the horse and gave him oats and hay, and then set up his stall against the gate of the sheriff's castle, crying, 'Pots for sale! Pots for sale! Buy a potty and get one free!' And soon a great crowd of wives and matrons gathered around him.

'Great bargains!' shouted Robin. 'Everything must go! I'm robbin' meself blind here! Buy a pot and get four free! Come on! I'm not standing here all day!' And everyone swore he hadn't been selling pots for long – for the pots that were worth 5 sold for 3 and the pots that were worth 3 were given away with the ones that were worth 5 but sold for 3, and even then you could do a deal with him.

There was an uproar and Robin sold fast and loud until he had only five pots left. Then the sheriff's wife looked out of her window to see what all the noise was and when she saw the mad potter she laughed and called down, 'What have you got for me today, potter?' Robin grinned up at her and said, 'My Lady, I've saved my best for you!' So she bade him come up and he took the five pots up to her chamber and gave them to her freely.

'Grammercy, sir,' she said eagerly, 'I'd have even more of you, for I *love* the look of your goods.'

'You shall have the best service I can offer,' said Robin, 'and I swear by Our Lady that I will be true to you.'

'Ah!' she cried, 'and today you shall have lunch with the sheriff and me.'

'God's mercy!' said Robin, 'But your bedding – I mean bidding – shall be done.'

And an hour later Robin and the Sheriff's wife went down to dinner.

When Robin came into the hall he bumped into the Sheriff, who had just come home from dispensing injustice in the courtroom, but then the Sheriff's wife swept in, clutching the pots and crying, 'Look, sir, what this kind potter has given us – so I said he could stay to dinner.'

'He's – er – welcome,' said the Sheriff, a bit confused, but his wife was a law unto herself and he no longer questioned what she did. And when they had washed and sat down to eat a most noble lunch indeed – a meal that Robin had never heard of – the Sheriff's men talked of the afternoon's shooting match and the wager laid thereon: 40 shillings going to the winner.

That made the potter sit up and when they had eaten their fill they made straight for the butts, the targets set up on the green outside the castle, with their best bows and arrows. The Sheriff's men shot fast and furiously, but they had all drunk too much at dinner and none of them got anywhere near the bull.

'By Our Lady!' said the potter, 'if I had a bow, thee'd see some shooting.' The Sheriff's men laughed but the Sheriff said, 'Lend him a bow – he's a stalwart sort of fellow, we'll try him out.'

One of the soldiers lent the potter a bow and, as he pulled the bowstring back to his ear, he muttered under his breath, 'Bloody hell, this is rubbish, no wonder we win all the time.' Then he carefully loosed an arrow, which thudded into the target a whole foot from the bull. The Sheriff's men guffawed and so, when the potter asked if he could join in the wager, they all agreed.

Then they all shot in turn until, by some miracle, the only ones left in the contest were the captain of the Sheriff's guard and the potter, more by luck than judgement, said the rest. It was time now to shoot at the willow wand from 100 paces. The captain went first.

His first arrow missed by a foot, the second by an inch, and the third actually nicked the wand, for he was a good archer and he had sobered up a bit by this time.

Then the potter took aim and now they all saw that there was something quite different in his concentrated stillness. His three arrows all cleft the wand, the first at the top, the second halfway down and the third where the wand entered the earth. The Sheriff's men were silent, thinking it a bitter shame to be beaten by a mere potter, but the Sheriff laughed at them and cried, 'Potter, you're the only man here worthy to bend a bow!'

'Well,' said the potter in the Sheriff's ear, after pocketing the 40 shillings, 'don't spread it around, in case the authorities get to hear of it, but the man who taught me to shoot was none other than Robin Hood.'

'You know Robin Hood?' said the Sheriff, aghast.

'Ssshh!' hissed Robin conspiratorially. 'Aye, I've shot with him many a time int' forest.'

'I'd give £100,' whispered the Sheriff, 'to have that false outlaw standing next to me.'

'Um, yes, well,' said the potter, 'if thou wilt dare to boldly go where no Norman has dared to go before, and if thou wilt give me £100, then tomorrow morning, before breakfast, thou'lt be face to face, man to man, sort of, with Robin Hood.'

'By Him that died on tree,' swore the Sheriff, 'I will reward you well for it.' Then they went back inside the castle, where supper and the Sheriff's wife awaited them.

❧

In the morning, at first light, they got ready to ride, the potter on his horse and cart, the Sheriff on his fine, black, Arab mare.

'Um, shouldn't we be taking some men with us?' suggested the Sheriff.

'Oh no,' said the potter, shaking his head seriously. 'Wi' a hundred clanking soldiers trampling through the forest, thee wouldn't see Robin at all – that's always been thy mistake – but I know where he goes when he wants to get away from his Merry Men, when they're being a bit too merry – it's a lovely little glade just at the edge of the forest with a lovely little brook tumbling through it. We'll find him there alone, as like as not, and then it'll be just thee and him, like.'

'What about you?' said the Sheriff.

'Oh, I'll be there,' said Robin. 'Um, look, Sheriff, um, you go on ahead, there's summat wrong wi' this harness, I'll catch thee up in half a tick.' And as the Sheriff trotted out through the castle gate, his wife slipped out through a side door, clad only in her white silk nightgown.

'My Lady,' said Robin, taking her in his arms, 'for my love, and this you were right well, I give you now this golden ring.'

'And I give this ring to you, brave Robin,' murmured the Sheriff's wife, 'and may Our Lady Mary keep you safe.' So they embraced and kissed and parted in the misty, early morning light with a soft, rosy fitter. Then Robin drove off after the Sheriff and together they made for Sherwood Forest. As they rode under the green leaves, each bird sang sweetly to its mate – cuckoo, cuckoo! And great joy was in the morning air and the Sheriff's heart leaped to see the beauty of the forest. Robin said, 'Aye, the forest is a lovely place on a summer's morning, especially for a man who can afford lodgings in the winter.' Then he drew a silver hunting horn from the cart, set it to his lips, and blew a blast that set the woodlands ringing. His men heard it from deep within the wood and they ran towards the sound – and when they reached the glade, the Sheriff was sitting on a stump with his head in his hands, while Robin was playing with his sword.

Little John laughed to see such fun and said, 'Did you sell all the pots, Master?'

'Oh yes,' said Robin, 'and look what I got for them – the Sheriff himself.'

'It's lovely to have him here,' said Little John.

'Doooh!' growled the Sheriff. 'Had I known who you were, you'd never have left Nottingham.'

'Aye,' said Robin, 'and do you think to leave the greenwood? Give me the £100 you owe me, and your horse and all your gear, and leave you shall.'

'Er, you will allow me my clothes?' stammered the Sheriff.

'Hmmmm, come to think of it, no,' said Robin. 'Looks like good gear. So get 'em off. Hither you came in all your privilege – naked shall you go home on foot. And when you get home, greet your wife well – she's a good woman and if it weren't for her, you should sing of more sorrow than this. I shall send her a white palfrey, gentle to ride.'

So the Sheriff made his way naked to Nottingham, creeping along ditches and hedges like a fugitive. Near the town he stole some peasant-woman's rags from a washing line and so entered Nottingham as a thieving beggar in drag. His wife greeted him at the castle gate, trying not to laugh.

'Sir! How fared you in the greenwood? Saw you Robin Hood?'

'Devil take him, body and soul!' cried the Sheriff. 'I have had a great humiliation, My Lady – he took everything from me: money, horse, weapons, even the clothes I stood up in.'

At that moment a small white horse trotted in through the castle gates and nuzzled the Sheriff's wife's hand.

'Aaaah!' cried the Sheriff in real fear. 'This is the white palfrey he said he'd send you! Now why the devil should he do that?' But his wife laughed loud and long, and when she'd done and wiped the tears from her eyes, she said, 'By Our Lady, you have paid well for that which Robin Hood gave to me – I mean the pots, of course. But come. Now you are safe home in Nottingham, you shall have goods enough.' And she took her bewildered husband by the hand and led him into the castle.

But now we will speak of Robin Hood and the potter, where they stood under the greenwood tree.

'Much,' said Robin, 'how much were the pots worth that I took to Nottingham?'

'Two nobles,' said the potter. (That's 13*s* 4*d* in the new money.)

'You shall have £10 for them,' said Robin, taking it from the Sheriff's purse. 'And now, Much the Miller's Son, say goodbye to the pottery and hello to the life of an outlaw!'

Thes partyd Robyn, the screffe and the pottere
Ondernethe the grenewode tre
God haffe mersey on Robyn Hodys solle
And saffe all god yemanry.

Three

Robin Hood and Guy of Gisborne

When shawes beene sheene and shradds full fayre
And leaves both large and longe
Itt is merry, walking in the fayre fforest
To heare the small birds songe.

The woodweele sang and wolde not cease
Amongst the leaves a lyne
And it is by two wight yeomen
By deare God that I meane ...

The sunlight slanted through the forest, catching every leaf on every tree in a halo of light and, as Robin walked here in the heart of the greenwood, his own heart was lightened by the sweet music of the birds. Above all, a robin sang without cease from the green depths of the wood until his heart was light as leaf on tree – when suddenly two strong men stepped from behind a tree and seized him. They took away his bow, beat him half senseless and bound him with thick, hard ropes. They spat on him and kicked him as he lay in the leaf-mulch. Squinting up through the red pain, he saw that one was his old enemy, the Sheriff of Nottingham, while the other was clad in a horse's hide, the head covering his head, the mane tumbling down his back, the tail dangling on the ground behind him, and he felt a tide of atavistic terror as if some ancient horse-god had come to devour him. This oddly garbed fellow was throwing a rope over a bough and he knew then that this was the moment of his death. At this point he focussed on the leaves, sticks and earth that were an inch from his right eye until they seemed huge, so huge that he could surely walk along that shrivelled brown leaf, swing himself down from its crinkled edge and lose himself in the infinitesimal tangle. He had almost done it too, when a hand was shaking his shoulder and, sitting up with a start, he found himself looking into the honest brown eyes of his giant-friend Little John.

Little John had never seen his little friend Robin Hood in such a state – wild-eyed, sweating and shuddering like a stuck pig, almost beside himself with fear and anger. Robin told John of his nightmare: 'I thought they beat me and bound me and took my bow from me – and as true as I am Robin Hood, alive now in this land, I'll be revenged upon them both!'

John tried to calm him. 'Dreams are not real, Master – they are but fleeting things, as the wind that blows the grass upon a hill, for if it be never so loud this night, tomorrow it may be still.' But the dream was real enough to Robin and he leaped to his feet.

'Arm yourselves, my Merry Men! Our enemies are near! But you, John, shall go with me, for we shall seek out these two men in the heart of the greenwood, wherever they may be!' And they put on their gowns and hoods of Lincoln green and, taking their longbows in their hands and their quivers full of bright arrows, they plunged into the forest, like swimmers into a green sea, and ran – skirting thickets, leaping over streams, panting up steep banks and racing like deer through the sun-slanted glades – until they came to those secret places wherein they took most delight, the sanctuaries of the deep forest; and there they stopped, for just ahead of them, they were aware of a man leaning against a tree. He wore a sword and dagger by his side and had a longbow in his hand, and he was clad in a horse's hide, the head covering his head, the mane tumbling down his back, the tail dangling on the ground behind him.

Robin stared at this weird figure white-faced, as if he was seeing a ghost, and he started trembling all over. Little John looked at him, amazed, and whispered, 'Stay here, Master, under this tree, and I will go to this strange fellow and find out what he's up to.' Robin turned to Little John, his face a blotch of fear and fury.

'Aaaah, John!' he gasped. 'You set no store by me and that's a wondrous strange thing! How often do I send my men ahead and stay behind myself? There's no cunning in knowing a villain if a man but hear him speak. You insult me, you overgrown lout, and if I didn't value my bow, I'd break it over your head!' But hasty words often breed misery and Little John hissed back, 'If that's how you feel about it, you can deal with old horsey-chops by yourself and I'll go back to camp!' And he parted from Robin and walked back to Barnsdale on paths well known to him.

But when he came to the outlaws' camp in Barnsdale, his heart sank like a stone, for there he found two of his comrades, the lookouts, slain in the forest glade bordering the camp – hacked to death – and the whole place was swarming with the Sheriff's men. But there was Will Scarlet, broken free of his captors, his red-hosed feet fair flying over stocks and stones, and the Sheriff himself reining his great warhorse round to go after him. Seven of the Sheriff's men were already hard at his heels, with one young fellow, William a Trent, gaining fast.

'One shot I'll shoot,' said Little John, 'that, by Christ's might and main, will make that fleeing fellow both glad and grateful.' He stood on the bank overlooking the camp and bent his bow of yew but, even as the arrow sped on its way, the bow, which was made of young wood, split in two and fell at his feet.

'Curse the wood!' cried Little John. 'And curse the tree it grew on! For this day you work my woe that should have been my friend!' But the arrow, though it was but loosely shot, flew through the air and met the Sheriff's man it was meant to meet, and William a Trent stood still, looking down in shock at the arrow that suddenly protruded from his throat. William a Trent's last thought was that he wished he had been very ill that day and had had to stay at home in bed, for that would have been better than standing here in the greenwood with an arrow through his throat. Then he fell and his eyes never saw this world again.

But the other six men who had been chasing Will Scarlet now turned on Little John and overpowered him – just, with the aid of several dozen others – and tied him to a tree. The Sheriff rode up on his horse. Little John stood so tall that they saw eye to eye with each other.

'You'll be dragged over dale and down,' sneered the Sheriff, 'and you'll be hanged high on a hill, that all the countryside may see. And before you're dead, we'll take you down and draw out your entrails round the shaft of a pike, and then we'll saw you slowly into quarters and each quarter will be hung up in a quarter of the shire, that men may be reminded that CRIME DOESN'T PAY.'

'Aye, 'appen you will,' said John, 'but if it's not Christ's will, 'appen you won't.'

But let us leave talking of Little John, for he is bound fast to a tree, so he's no fun any more, and we will talk of Robin Hood and the stranger in the horse-hide, who stood in the heart of the greenwood. We will see how these two stout yeomen met under the russet leaves of autumn, and learn the business they had with each other at that time. Robin stepped forward and showed himself.

'Good morrow, good fellow,' said the man, in the sneering voice of a Norman overlord addressing a Saxon serf. 'I should guess by the bow that you bear in your hand that you're a good archer and a forester.' Robin nodded. The man went on: 'I seem to have mislaid my way and have lost track of the time. Do you know these parts well? Do you come here often?'

'I'll lead you through the wood,' said Robin. 'Good fellow, I'll be your guide; but where do you want to go?'

I'm looking for an outlaw,' said the man, stepping away from the tree. 'Men call him Robin Hood and I'd rather meet up with him today than have £40 in gold.'

'Why do you want to meet with Robin Hood?' said Robin Hood. 'Most men try to avoid him.'

'Ah!' breathed the man. 'Scum like Robin Hood are like cream to me. Their death is my living and the Sheriff of Nottingham will pay well for the head of Robin Hood.'

'And what's the Sheriff doing while you're doing his job for him?' Robin wanted to know.

'The Sheriff is even now attacking the outlaws' camp,' boasted the man, 'acting on information that I myself tortured out of an old peasant woman. But Robin Hood is a wily fox and will escape. He'll come here to the heart of the greenwood and I'll show him who is the master in this land.'

'Well,' said Robin, 'if you two met, it would soon be seen who was the better man before you parted, but let us find some other pastime, good fellow, I pray you. Let us make trials of our skill as we walk in the woods and, who knows, we may even chance to meet with Robin Hood in an unexpected moment.'

They cut down two thin saplings growing among the briars and set them up together at a range of 60 roods (or 330 yards), attaching a garland of wildflowers around the tips.

'Lead on, good fellow,' said the man in the horse-hide. 'Lead on, I do implore you.'

'Nay, by my faith,' said Robin Hood. 'You lead on first.'

The man's first shot whistled past the garland an inch wide of the mark. Robin's first shot rattled the flowers. The man's second shot also pierced the garland. He was a damn good archer. But Robin's second shot clove his sapling in two. The man's third shot nicked his sapling but Robin's third shot also clove his, further down.

'God bless your heart!' cried the man. 'That was a good shot! And if your heart is as good as your hands, then you're a better man than Robin Hood. But come, tell me your name, good fellow.'

'Not till you've told me yours,' said Robin.

'I dwell by dale and down,' said the man, 'for I travel a lot. My work is killing people that other people don't want alive, and I'm very good at it. The Sheriff will give me a knight's ransom for the head of Robin Hood. He that calls me by my right name calls me Sir Guy of Gisborne, and my sword and dagger have been the untimely death of many a man – aye, and woman and child too.'

'My dwelling is here in the wood,' said Robin, his eyes blazing, 'and I don't give a tinker's turd for the likes of you.

You Norman bastards are all the same – mercenary, ruled by greed – you're the biggest thieves in the world. Well, my name is Robin Hood of Barnsdale, and I gather you've been looking for me.'

Then, provided you weren't closely related to either of them, you would have enjoyed the show, as these two fellows went at it together with bright and gleaming blades. Two hours of a hot, early autumn day they fought, and neither of them gave an inch of ground. Sir Guy had the weight and Robin was nimble – but not so nimble after two hours of hot, fierce work, and all at once he tripped on a root. This time Guy was quick and struck him a blow on the left side. Robin rolled but Guy's sword swung up for the death-stroke, the sun catching it in a halo of light, and Robin's mind caught a fleeting image of the Virgin Mary.

'Dear Lady!' he cried within, 'that art both mother and maid! It was never a man's destiny to die before his day!' And he scrambled up with an awkward, back-handed stab that sent the point of his sword into Guy's heart. Sir Guy fell and lay still, looking surprised. Robin cut off Sir Guy's head and, holding it by the hair, thrust it onto the end of his bow, saying, 'You've been a traitor all your life but now here's an end to it.' Then he pulled out his Irish hunting knife and went to work with it on Sir Guy's face until no one, not even Sir Guy's mother, could have told who he was. He laid the head upon the ground and said, 'Lie there now, lie there, good Sir Guy, and don't be angry with me. As you've had the worse cuts at my hand, so you shall have the better clothes.' And he stripped himself and Sir Guy's dead body and dressed Guy's body in his own gown and hood of Lincoln green, and he put on that horse's hide that covered him from head to foot and he pulled the horse's head down over his head, like a mask, and peered out through the empty sockets. Then he pulled his lips back and grinned and snarled like a wild beast. 'I'll take thy bow, thy arrows and thy horn too,' he murmured, 'for I'd best get back to camp to see how my men are doing.'

The Sheriff had found a small hill close to the edge of Sherwood Forest and on the top of the hill was a single beech tree. From one of the boughs depended a taut rope, the end of which made a tight noose round Little John's bull-like neck – but the Sheriff was evidently waiting for something. Even Little John was beginning to wish they'd get on with it, when at last they heard a loud blast on a horn just inside the tree-cover and the Sheriff leaped to his feet, for he had been sitting on a rock at the foot of the hill.

'Hah! Hah!' he cried. 'Listen to that! That is good music and it brings good tidings, for that is Sir Guy's horn and it means he has slain Robin Hood. And see! Here comes that fearful fighter, clad in his horse's hide. By God's nails, he looks even more sinister than ever. And see! There! On his bow's end – the head of Robin Hood!'

The entire company fell silent at the approach of that awful figure with the mutilated head on the end of its bow. Little John's heart sank like a stone down a cold well and he wished he were dead. He thought that wish would soon be granted.

'Come hither, good Sir Guy!' brayed the Sheriff. 'Ask of me whatsoever you will have.'

'I'll none of your gold,' said the horse-head in a strange, muffled voice, 'but now that I have slain the master, let me go and kill his man – that is all I ask and no more will I have.'

'You're a madman!' said the Sheriff. 'You'd have had a knight's ransom for killing Robin Hood! But, since that's all you ask, I grant it readily.' His Norman greed had overcome his common sense, which should have told him that this was a little out of character for Sir Guy of Gisborne.

But Little John had heard his master's voice and thought, 'Now shall I escape, by Christ's might in heaven.' Robin threw the grisly head at the Sheriff's feet, making him hop, and splattering his boots, and hurried up the hill towards Little John. The Sheriff and his soldiers kept close company.

'Stand back!' snarled Robin. 'Why draw so near to me? It was never the custom in our country to hear another's shrift!' They held back, so much in awe were they of this sinister assassin, and Robin drew his Irish knife and pretended to wound John horribly while John writhed and screamed. But he loosed him hand and foot and put Sir Guy's bow into his hand. John fitted an arrow to the string – seeing with horror that the tips of all Sir Guy's arrows were rusty with dried blood – and the Sheriff and his men stared with terror at this sudden apparition of the two greatest archers in England, bows in hand, a full quiver apiece, standing against them at point-blank range.

They turned and ran but Robin Hood and Little John shot them down, in the back, two by two, as fast as you could count – and the Sheriff? Well:

> He cold neither soe fast goe
> Nor away soe fast cold runn,
> But Litle John, with an arrow broade,
> Did shoote him in the bumm.

And a long time was the Sheriff recovering from that one. But Robin Hood and Little John went wearily back into the greenwood to pick up the pieces of their precarious outlaw life.

Four

Robin Hood's
Death

The day came when the king himself entered the forest and persuaded Robin Hood to give up his precarious outlaw's life, and Robin Hood and his Merry Men left the greenwood and took service with the king in London. But they had only been at the court for a year and three months before all their money was gone and only two of Robin's men still stood by him – Little John and Will Scarlet. All three of them were heartily sick of the life at court: the greed, the waste, the hypocrisy, the obscene panting after privilege – *plus ça change*, pardon my French!

One day Robin was watching some boys shooting at targets on Tower Green, down by the River Thames. It was a lovely autumn day, fresh and cold, a pale sun hovering over the mists of the river.

'Alas!' said Robin, 'all my money is spent and the thing I do best is counted for nothing here – mere sport for boys. Once I was a good archer, happen the best in England. Alas and well-away! If I stay any longer here in London with the king, sorrow itself will surely slay me.'

So Robin went to the king, bowed down upon one knee, and said, 'My lord king, in Sherwood I built a little chapel, dedicated to Mary Magdalene. I long with all my heart to go there for one last time to do penance for my many great sins, or remorse and guilt will surely slay me.'

'Very well,' said Edward our comely king, 'I give you leave of absence for seven nights. No longer must you dwell away from me, on pain of death.'

'Thank you, My Lord,' said Robin, bowing low. Then, his heart as light as leaf on tree, he hurried to his chamber, where Little John and Will Scarlet were waiting, dressed as usual in the royal livery but with green bundles on their backs. Robin took a green bundle from his chest and they made their way to the stables, where they saddled their horses and rode merrily out of London town.

North up Watling Street they rode and when at last they rode in under the green leaves of Sherwood and heard the birds singing sweetly, Robin Hood said, 'It's a long time since I was here. I think it would do me good to shoot one of the king's deer.' So Robin stalked and shot a great red hart and blew his horn till the whole forest rang. The outlaws of the forest knew that horn and came running to gather in the glade where Robin stood, about 100 strong bowmen, and they doffed their hoods and went down on one knee, as if Robin had been the king himself.

'Welcome home!' they cried. 'Lord of the Greenwood!' And Robin Hood lived in Sherwood for another twenty-two years and, for fear of Edward our comely king, he never left the greenwood again.

But Robin was betrayed in his last days by his own cousin, the Prioress of Kirklees, for the sinful love she bore a certain knight, Sir Roger of Doncaster, devil take them both! They plotted together as they lay naked in the Prioress's bed, to slay Robin Hood for the reward money placed on his head by the king.

Robin was getting old now, and one winter's day he was taken ill with a fever. He said to Little John as they huddled in a hollow filled with dead leaves, 'You know, John, we two have shot for many a shilling but I can't shoot now – my broad arrows no longer fly true. But my cousin, the Prioress of Kirklees, has sent to say that she will bleed me, to bring this fever down so I'll be able to shoot again.'

'I wouldn't go there, Master,' said Will Scarlet, 'not without a dozen good bowmen, for there's a fellow at Kirklees who will quarrel with you, and you're in no condition to fight.' Robin's hot temper flared up at once.

'D'you think I fear Red Roger of Doncaster?' he cried. 'But if you're afraid of him, William Scarlet-Pants, then you'd better stay here!'

'Sorry I spoke,' said Will, 'but don't get cross; I won't say another word.'

'You know,' said Much the Miller's Son, 'a nice haunch of venison would do you good, along with a few quarts of ale.'

'No,' said Robin, 'I will not eat and I will not drink until I have been to Kirklees Priory and got some of this hot blood out of my veins, and no man shall go with me but Little John.'

'Aye, well, mind you don't quarrel with him,' muttered Will Scarlet, but Robin did not hear.

◁

So Robin Hood and Little John went on their
way through the woods until they came to a
black water, an evil, stinking bog, over which
lay a series of wooden planks. On one of these
planks there squatted an old woman, a hide-
ous crone with a nose like a sickle, dressed in
foul black rags; and she was cursing Robin
Hood, over and over again, all the while stab-
bing a green effigy with a long red pin.

'Why do you curse Robin Hood?' said
Robin. 'And who has paid you to do so?'

'A noble lady,' croaked the crone, looking
up sly and askance, so that Robin shuddered
and crossed his fingers against her.

'But I love all women,' said he, 'even you,
for the sake of Mild Mary.' The old hag cack-
led and shuffled back across the planks and
vanished in the evil mist surrounding the
bog. And Robin and Little John crossed the
black water and went on their way through
the woods until they came to a grove of silver

birch trees hard by Kirklees Priory – and here were three young women, all in white, kneeling and weeping and praying for the soul of Robin Hood.

'Why do you weep for Robin Hood?' said Robin. 'And who has paid you to pray for him?'

'A noble lady,' they said, 'and we weep for his body that today will lose its blood.' But Robin said, 'The Prioress is my aunt's daughter, my cousin, and once upon a time she loved me dearly. She would not harm me for the world.' But the women went on weeping and praying.

And Robin Hood and Little John went on then without pause to Kirklees Priory and knocked upon the door-pin. The Prioress opened the door and let Robin in, but bade Little John wait outside. John was loath to do so, but Robin ordered him to obey. And the Prioress led Robin into the hall where she kissed him tenderly and said, 'Please sit down, cousin Robin, and drink some wine with me for old times' sake.'

But Robin said, 'No, I will not eat and I will not drink until you have bled me and got this hot blood out of my veins.'

'Well,' said she, 'I have a little room, cousin Robin, which you have never seen. It is a private room and it is there that I shall bleed you, for I would not have everyone know that I entertain the famous outlaw.' And she took him by his fevered hand and led him to that little room, where a bare bed lay against one wall and a good warm fire burned in the grate. There she bade him lie upon the bed while she fetched the instruments. Almost at once she returned with a pair of blood-irons, or lancing-knives, wrapped in silk, and a chafing-dish full of water, for heating them.

'I'll set the chafing-dish to the fire,' said the Prioress, 'while you roll up your sleeve.' Now, he is an unwise man that heeds no warnings. When the blood-irons were ready, she laid them to a large vein in Robin's wrist and – alas for pity! She pierced the vein and held it open and let out the blood; it was a rich deep red as it dropped steadily into the bowl by the bed. Robin lay back and closed his eyes and the Prioress slipped softly from the room and locked the door without making a sound.

All that day Robin bled, and first he bled the thick, thick blood and then he bled the thin, and then Robin Hood knew well there was treachery within. And as if from a great distance he heard Little John's voice: 'Are you well, Master?'

He replied, 'In faith, John, not very well.' But it was no more than a whisper.

All this time Little John had stood outside the door, despairing, for he did not know what to do. Suddenly, a man rushed at him from the trees, a heavyset man with red hair, clad all in black. John turned but the man thrust a dagger into his ribs. John, though a giant, was light of foot and he leaped to one side, whipping out his sword and slicing it sideways into the man's neck, almost decapitating him. The man fell and quivered violently, his blood pumping into the ground.

'Lie there, Red Roger!' gasped Little John. 'Lie there for the dogs to eat!' Then he broke in the door with three great blows. The priory was empty, and John ran like a madman through all the echoing rooms and corridors until he came to a low, locked door, which he kicked in with one blow. And so he came to where Robin lay, white as death upon the bed, the whole floor covered in red, where it had overflowed the bowl. John fell to his knees in this rich, red carpet by the bed and Robin slowly turned his chalk-white face to him.

'Give me communion, John,' he whispered, 'with your own hand. I trust Almighty God to shrive me of my sins.' And when John had given him both bread and wine, he said, 'Now for Christ's love, Master, give me leave to set fire to this unholy place and burn it to the ground.'

'No,' breathed Robin, 'I cannot give you leave for that, John. I never hurt a woman in my life and if I should do so now at the end of it, God would blame me. But give me my best bow in my hand and one more arrow I'll let fly. And where you take this arrow up, there shall you let me lie; and set my bright sword at my head, my arrows at my feet and lay my yew-bow at my side, which was my music sweet.'

And Little John placed the bow in Robin's hand, closing his huge brown fist over Robin's white one; and he notched a broad fair arrow to the string and, closing his fingers round Robin's, he pulled the string back as far as he could, for Robin's strength was all gone. He took aim and let fly and the arrow winged its way through the small window on the other side of the room and flew merrily into the greenwood.

Robin died there and then and Little John took his body up in his arms, for he was now as light as leaf on tree, and bore him into the greenwood. He buried him at the place where his last arrow had fallen.

So died the great English outlaw. But if anyone can be said to live forever, it is surely Robin Hood.

Five

A Lytell Geste of Robyn Hode

Lythe and listin, gentilmen
That be of frebore blode;
I shall you tel of a gode yeman,
His name was Robyn Hode.

[Open your ears and listen / Ladies and gents of freeborn blood / I shall tell of a good yeoman / His name was Robyn Hode.]

The First Fytte

Robin was a proud outlaw while he walked the earth; there was never found on English ground so courteous an outlaw as he. One day Robin stood in Barnsdale, leaning against a tree. At his side stood Little John – he was a good yeoman, all 6ft 7in of him. By them stood Will Scarlet and Much the Miller's Son – there wasn't an inch of his 5ft 1in that wasn't worth a man.

Then spoke Little John to Robin Hood: 'Master, it would do you good to dine on time.' And his stomach gave out a mighty rumble, as if a thunderstorm threatened the peace of the forest. Robin said, 'I'll not dine until I have some bold baron or some other unknown guest – some knight or squire dwelling here in the west – that can afford to pay for a slap-up meal.'

Robin had a good custom at that time: every day before he dined, he would hear three Masses – one for the Father, one for the

Holy Ghost and one for Our Dear Lady, whom he loved the most; for Robin loved Mary the Mother of God more dearly than Father, Son and Holy Ghost put together, and for fear of committing a deadly sin, he would never harm any company that a woman was in.

'Master,' said Little John, wearily resigned, 'before we spread our board, and may that noble act be not long in coming, tell us how to proceed and what life to lead: what to take, what to leave, who to reive and who to beat and bind.'

'It's no great matter,' said Robin, 'we'll do well enough. But make sure you harm no common husbandman who tills the land with his plough. No more shall you hurt any good yeoman or peasant that walks by the greenwood thickets, nor no knight nor squire that is an honest fellow. But these bishops and these archbishops – them must you rob and reive – these fat clerics, these flabby abbots, that get rich on the backs of the poor, these portly robber barons, these Norman bastards, forgive the tautology, these usurers and fat-cat money-merchants – them you must beat and bind – and the high and mighty Sheriff of Nottingham, bear him well in mind!'

'We shall hold by this word,' said Little John, 'and we'll learn our lesson well. And now that here endeth the lesson and it's so far on in the day, God send us a guest, so that we can be at our dinner!'

'Well,' said Robin, 'take your bow in hand – Much and Will Scarlet can go with you, let no man abide with me – and walk up to the Sayles on Watling Street and wait for an unknown guest that you meet there by chance. And be he earl, baron, abbot or knight, bring him home to me and I'll have his dinner ready.'

So these three yeomen walked up to the Sayles Plantation on the northern edge of Barnsdale Forest, 500 yards east of Wentbridge, and there, on this elevated vantage point, they looked east and west and saw no one; but as they looked back into Barnsdale, down a secret way, they saw a knight riding towards them and quickly they went to meet him. But when they came up to him, they saw at once that his appearance was dreary and that he had little self-esteem; one foot stood in the stirrup, the other dangled beside. His hood hung down over his eyes and he was arrayed very poorly; a sorrier-looking man never rode on a summer's day.

But Little John was full of courtesy and bent down on one knee: 'Most welcome you are, gentle knight, most welcome you are to me, most gracious and noble knight. My master has waited for you, fasting, good sir, for a full three hours now.'

'Who is your master?' said the knight.

'Robin Hood,' said John.

'He is an honest yeoman,' said the knight. 'I have heard much good said of him so I'll go with you, my brothers, though my intention today was to have dined at Blyth or Doncaster.'

This gentle knight went with them then, a troubled look clouding his face, for the tears ran out of his eyes like rain and fell down his cheeks. They brought him to the door of the forest lodge and when Robin saw him, he courteously doffed his hood and went down on his knee.

'Welcome, sir knight,' said Robin, 'I have waited for you, fasting sir, these three hours long.'

Then answered the gentle knight with words both fair and frank. 'God save thee, good Robin, and all thy fair company.'

Then they washed and wiped themselves and sat down to dinner and Little John was never so happy in his life. They had plenty of bread and wine and choice cuts of venison; swan and pheasant they had in plenty and river fowl too, and all kinds of little birds that breed on the branches.

'Dig in with a will, sir knight,' said Robin.

'Grammercy, sir,' said he. 'I've not had such a dinner as this for the past three weeks. If I ever come again, Robin, into your country, I'll treat you to as good a dinner as you have treated me.'

'Grammercy, knight,' said Robin. 'When I have my dinner, I am never so greedy, by God, as to crave for it. This feast was freely given – you don't have to pay it back. But you can pay *for* it before you go. I reckon that's only right, for it was never the custom, by God, for a yeoman to pay for a knight.'

'For my shame,' said the knight, 'I have nothing in my coffers that I may offer you.'

'Go and look, Little John,' said Robin, 'and don't hang back out of politeness. Now tell me the truth, sir knight, as God will save your soul.'

'I have no more than ten shillings,' said the knight, 'so God save my soul.'

'Well, if you really have no more,' said Robin, 'I won't take a single penny. And if you have need of more, I'll gladly lend you some. Go now, Little John, and tell me the truth – if there's no more than ten bob, I'll not take a penny of it.'

Little John spread his cloak upon the ground and there he found in the knight's coffers no more than half a pound. He let it lie there nice and still and went to his master and bowed.

'Well, John,' said Robin, 'what's the news?'

'Sir,' he said, 'the knight is true enough.'

'Fill our cups with the best wine,' said Robin, 'and then the knight will begin his story. For I did wonder greatly, sir knight, why your clothing is so worn and thin. Just tell me one thing – and I'll keep it to myself – but I think you were compelled to be a knight. You were a yeoman who got too successful and had land worth more than £40 so they made you a knight to swell the ranks of Edward's army and tax you at a higher rate –'

'No, no, Robin,' interrupted the knight. 'It was nothing to do with "distraint of knighthood" –'

'Or else,' went on Robin, 'you've managed your affairs badly – lived in strife with your neighbours, got into debt, relied on usurers, spent all your money on luxury and lechery, led a life of sin –'

'By God that made me!' cried the knight, almost in tears at Robin's hard words, 'I am none of these! My ancestors have been knights in the North Country for over 100 years. But it often happens, Robin, that a man may fall on hard times and lose his status – though even then God who sits in heaven above may amend his state. Within these two years, Robin, and you can ask my neighbours, I could have spent £400 of good money every year. Now I have nothing but my wife and children, for God has shaped it so for me.'

'How did you lose your riches?' asked Robin.

'By my folly and my soft heart,' he said. 'To tell the truth, Robin, I had a son who should have been my heir, but when he was just twenty years old he got in with the jousting set, and tournaments and mock battles were all he cared for. But then he killed a knight of Lancaster and his squire too, and to save him from death and buy a pardon for him I have had to sell all my goods and pledge my lands as security to a rich abbot in these parts, the abbot of St Mary's Abbey in York. And now I am riding to St Mary's to hand over my land to him.'

'Tell me true,' said Robin, 'what is the sum?'

'Sir,' he said, with tears in his eyes, '£400, according to the abbot.'

'And if you lose your lands,' said Robin, 'what will happen to you?'

'I'll have to busk it,' said the knight, 'and go over the salt sea to the place where Christ was both dead and alive on the mount of Calvary. In short, I'll go on the Crusades and try to recoup my fortunes in the Holy Land, for it'll not get any better for me here at home.' And tears fell from his eyes as he prepared to go on his way.

'Farewell, my friend,' he said, 'and have a good day, for I have no money to pay you.'

'Where are your friends?' said Robin.

'Oh, sir, not one of them wants to know me now! When I was rich enough in my castle at home they boasted loudly of my acquaintance, but now they run away from me as from a wild beast – or they ignore me and cut me dead, as if they did not see me.'

Then Little John wept for pity and Scarlet and Much kept him company.

'Fill our cups with the best wine!' cried Robin. 'To cheer us up. Now then, do you have a friend, sir knight, that would stand security for a loan?'

'I have no friend,' said the knight, 'but God that died on tree.'

'Away with your jokes!' cried Robin. 'Do you think I'd take God as your security, or St Peter or St Paul? Nay, by Him that made me and shaped both sun and moon, find me a better guarantor or you get no money from me!'

'I have no other,' said the knight sadly, 'unless it were Our Dear Lady – she never failed me yet.'

'By God,' said Robin in amazement, 'you could search the whole of England through and not find a guarantor more to my liking. So go to the treasury, Little John, and bring me £400 and make sure it's well counted.'

Little John and Scarlet went to the treasury and counted out £400.

'Is this well counted?' said Much the Miller's Son. 'It looks a hell of a lot.'

'What's bugging you?' said Little John. 'It's alms to help a gentle knight who has fallen on hard times. Master,' he went on, 'his clothing is threadbare. You must give the knight a livery to clothe his body decently, for you have scarlet cloth and green, and many a rich array – there's no richer merchant in the whole of England.'

'Give him three yards of every colour,' said Robin, 'and measure it well.' But Little John took no measuring stick but his bow, so with every handful he gave the knight an extra 3ft.

'What sort of devil's draper do you think you are?' said Much. Scarlet just stood and laughed.

'By God Almighty, John may well give him good measure, for it's not costing him a thing!'

'Master,' said Little John, 'Give the knight a horse to carry all this gear home with him.'

'Give him a grey courser,' said Robin, 'with a brand-new saddle, for he is Our Lady's messenger, so God grant that he be true.'

'Why not give him a good palfrey for his wife?' said Much, 'to keep up his new appearance?'

'And a new pair of boots,' said Scarlet, 'for he is now a very gentle knight.'

'And what shall you give him, Little John?' said Robin.

'Sir,' said John, 'a pair of spurs to spur him on his way and bring him swiftly out of his sorrow so that he may pray for all this generous company and pay us back.'

'When shall my day of repayment be?' said the knight.

'This day twelvemonth,' said Robin, 'under this very tree. But you know, it's a shame for a knight to ride alone, without squire or yeoman to walk by his side; so I shall lend you my man, Little John, and he shall be your yeoman, should you have need of one.' And Robin winked at Little John and

John scowled, but Scarlet and Much laughed long and loud, until Little John joined in and laughed the loudest. And so he and the knight went merrily on their way.

The Second Fytte

The knight, now gone on his way, looked back into Barnsdale and blessed Robin Hood and John, Much and Scarlet, for the best company he was ever in. Then that gentle knight said to Little John, 'Tomorrow I must be in York, at St Mary's Abbey, and to the abbot I must pay £400. And unless I get there tonight, my land is lost for ever.'

On the following day, in St Mary's Abbey in the city of York, the abbot was saying to his monks, 'This day twelvemonth Sir Richard At-the-Lea came here and borrowed £400 against all his lands; and unless he comes this very same day, he shall be disinherited.'

'It's quite early,' said the Prior. 'It's not yet far gone in the day. I'd rather pay £100 and sleep easy in my bed. Sir Richard is far beyond the sea, leaving his rightful estates in England, suffering cold and hunger and many a wretched night in our Dear Lord's service on the Crusades. It would be a great pity to get his lands like this – and if you are so light of conscience, you do him great wrong.'

'You are always in my beard!' roared the abbot. 'By God and St Richard of Chichester!' And with that, in came a fat-headed monk, the chief cellarer of the abbey.

'He's dead or hanged,' said the monk cheerfully. 'By God that bought me dear, we shall have £400 a year more to spend in this place.'

The abbot and the chief cellarer then boldly leapt up to greet the Lord Chief Justice of England, whom the abbot was putting up, for the Lord Chief Justice and many others had taken the knight's debt in hand, to stitch him up good and proper. The abbot and his company judged Sir Richard very hard: 'Unless he comes this very day, he shall be disinherited.'

'He will not come today, I dare well hazard,' said the justice; but in a sorrowful time for them all the knight was at the gate; and there Sir Richard Attlee said to his man, Little John, 'Let us put on our old, worn garments that we brought with us from the forest.' So they put on their old, worn garments and arrived at the gate, where the porter was ready to welcome them.

'Welcome, sir knight,' said the porter. 'My lord abbot is at dinner and so is many a gentleman, all for love of thee.' Then the porter swore a great oath, 'By God that made me, here are the best-built horses I ever saw and your fellow too – he's built like a horse himself. Lead them all into the stable, that they might be well looked after.' Little John looked at the porter but the knight stayed his hand.

'They'll not go into that stable,' said Sir Richard, 'by God that died on tree!'

The lords had all sat down to dine in that abbot's hall, when the knight and Little John came in and kneeled down and saluted them both high and low.

'I hope you are glad, sir abbot,' said Sir Richard, 'for I have come to keep my day.' But the first word the abbot spoke was, 'Have you brought my pay?'

'Not one penny,' said the knight, 'by God that made me.'

'You're a cursed debtor,' sneered the abbot. 'Now, sir justice, drink to me. So what are you doing here, if you haven't brought me my money?'

'For God's sake,' said Sir Richard, 'to beg for more time.'

'Your day is broken,' said the justice. 'You will have no land.'

'Now good sir justice!' cried Sir Richard. 'Be my friend and defend me from my enemies!'

'I hold with the abbot,' said the justice, 'for we are cut of the same cloth and are both in it for the money.'

'Now good sir sheriff, be my friend!' cried the knight.

'No, in God's name,' swore the Sheriff of Nottingham.

'Now good sir abbot, be my friend!' cried Sir Richard. 'For the sake of courtesy, hold my lands until I have £400 of good money for you.'

The abbot swore, 'By God, get the land where you will, you'll get none from me!'

'By dear God,' swore the knight, 'that wrought the whole world, unless I have my land again, it shall be very dearly bought and somebody will surely suffer for it. God, that was born of a maiden, grants us to look after ourselves; and a man in need soon finds out who his friends are.'

The abbot then looked on him with loathing and began to abuse him villainously. 'Out!' he cried. 'You false knight, get out of my hall at once!'

'You lie,' said the knight calmly. 'Abbot, in your own hall you lie. False knight I never was, by God that made us all.' Then Sir Richard Attlee stood up and said to the abbot, 'To suffer a knight to kneel so long proves that you have no courtesy or good manners. In jousts and tournaments I have been ever in the thick of it and put myself in as great danger as any that I ever saw.'

'What more will you give,' said the justice to the abbot, 'to make Sir Richard release his claim upon the land? Otherwise, I dare swear, you'll never hold the land in peace.'

'£100,' said the abbot.

'Give him £200,' said the justice.

'No, by God,' said Sir Richard. 'You won't get it like that. Though you gave me £1,000 more, you'd never be nearer to having it. My heirs will never be abbot, justice or sheriff.' Then he crossed the floor to a round table, where he shook exactly £400 out of a bag.

'Here, have your gold, sir abbot,' said the knight, 'Had you been courteous when I came here, you should have been rewarded with interest.'

The abbot sat still and ate no more, for all his royal fare. He dropped his head upon his chest and stared hard at the ground. 'Give me my gold again, sir justice,' muttered the abbot, 'that I gave to you.'

'Not a penny,' said the justice, 'by God that died on tree.'

'Sir sheriff,' murmured the abbot, 'give me my gold again that I gave to you.'

'Not one penny,' said the Sheriff, 'by God that died on tree.'

'Sir abbot and you men of law,' said Sir Richard, 'now I have held to my day and now I shall have my land again, for all that you can say.'

Sir Richard and Little John went out through the door – gone was all their care – and they put back on their fine clothing, while their old, worn garments they left at the gate. Then they rode away from St Mary's Abbey, singing merrily as they rode, as men have told in the old tale; and the knight's lady met them at the gate, back home in Wyresdale.

'Welcome, my lord,' said his lady. 'Sir – are all our possessions lost?'

'Be merry, dame,' said Sir Richard, 'and pray for Robin Hood, 'that ever his soul be in bliss. He helped me out of our trouble and if it hadn't been for his kindness, we would have been beggars. The abbot and I are quits; he's been given his pay, for the good yeoman Robin Hood lent it to me as I came by the way.' Little John went into the castle with them and served Sir Richard Attlee and his wife most faithfully for most of the following year; and the knight lived happily at home all that time, until he had saved up £400, all ready to pay his debt to Robin.

Then he had made 100 bows, the strings expertly fitted, and 100 sheaves of fine arrows, the heads burnished bright; and every arrow an ell long (that's 45in), superbly fitted with peacock feathers and worked with white silver – it was a splendid sight. He also hired 100 men, well-equipped with armour and weapons, with himself in the same colours, clothed in white and red. He bore a lance in his hand and a man led his packhorse

– not Little John, for he was no longer with
the knight, but more of him anon; and so
Sir Richard rode, with a light-hearted song,
towards Barnsdale.

But as he rode over the bridge at Wentbridge,
he saw a wrestling match taking place and he
stayed there to watch, for there were gathered all the best yeomen in the West Riding of
Yorkshire. A full fair game was there set up,
with magnificent prizes – a white bull, a great
courser with saddle and bridle of burnished
gold, a pair of gloves, a red-gold ring, a pipe of
wine – and whatever man bore himself the best
would bear the best prize away.

There was a yeoman in that place who
was the best of them all and won every single
match, but because he was a stranger from
foreign parts – that is, Lancashire – the locals
set about to slay him. Sir Richard had pity on
his countryman and swore that the yeoman
should not come to harm, for love of Robin
Hood. So he pressed into that place, with his
100 men following him, all with bent bows

and sharp arrows, to put that company to shame. His men shouldered everyone out of the way and made room for him, so that they should all hear what he had to say – and he took the yeoman by the hand and gave him all the prizes.

Then he gave the yeoman 5 marks for the wine (that's £3 6s and 8d in the new money) – the barrel sat there on the ground and he ordered it to be broached, that all who wished might drink. And so this gentle knight stayed a long time in that place, until the game was over; and all that time Robin waited, fasting for three whole hours of the afternoon.

The Third Fytte

Attend now and listen, good people – all that are still here, that is; of Little John, that had become the knight's man, you shall hear a merry tale. One fine day the young men of Sir Richard's household went to a shooting match held at Nottingham; so Little John fetched his bow and went with them. At the match Little John took three turns to shoot and each time he slit the wand, even though the Sheriff of Nottingham was standing by the marks, the silly sod. The sheriff swore a mighty oath. 'By Him that died on tree, this man is the best archer I ever saw! Tell me now, you brave young chap, what is your name? In what country were you born? And where do you dwell?'

'I was born in Holderness, sir, where me mum was living at the time, and men call me Reynold Greenleaf when I'm at home.'

'Tell me, Reynard Greenleaf, would you dwell with me? I would pay you 20 marks a year.'

'I have a master,' said Little John, 'a courteous knight. It'd be best if you got leave of him.'

The sheriff obtained Little John from the knight for a twelvemonth and Sir Richard gave Little John a good strong horse as a leaving present, 'in case you need a quick getaway'. And they both laughed long and heartily as John took his leave of the honest knight and his wife and rode out of Wyresdale in Lancashire to make his way to Nottingham over the Peak District.

❦

And now Little John is the sheriff's man, God help us! But he was always plotting how to pay him out, for, as he said, 'By the backs of God's knees, I'll be the worst servant he ever had!'

It so happened one Wednesday that the sheriff went hunting, leaving Little John still in bed. There he languished, fasting till it was past midday.

'Oi! Bar-steward!' then bawled Little John. 'It's a long time for Greenleaf to be fasting – therefore I pray you, sir bar-steward, bring me my dinner!'

'By God, you'll not eat nor drink,' called up the steward, 'till my lord comes home!'

'By God!' swore Little John, bounding out of bed and straight down the stairs, 'I'd rather crack your crown!' The steward was a rude curmudgeon and he stood his ground, leaping to the larder and shutting fast the door. But Little John gave him a gentle tap that near broke his back and, though the fellow should live for 100 years, he would hobble lamely. John kicked the pantry door wide open and brought out large quantities of ale and wine.

'Since you will not dine,' said John, 'I will give you to drink,' and he turned the steward onto his broken back and poured wine down his throat, until the poor fellow was all but drowned. Then Little John ate and drank, taking his time; but in that kitchen the sheriff had a cook, a stout and bold man, and he came in and saw the steward half dead on the floor and Little John on a stool, stuffing his face like a monk with an hour to live.

'By God's guts,' he said, 'you're the devil of a servant, serving yourself like this.' And he

lent Little John three hefty punches, knocking him off the stool.

'By God's ballocks,' said Little John, spit-
ting out teeth and bits of meat, 'those were
right good punches! I think you're a bold,
hardy man and, before I take my leave of
you, I'll put you to a better test.' And Little
John got to his feet and drew his sword.

'But I haven't got a sword!' cried the cook.
'I'm only a cook!'

'We'll see how good you are with mine,'
said Little John, and advanced upon the cook,
who scrabbled round the table and wrenched
out the steward's sword. Neither of them
thought to flee but stood face to face and then
they fought bitterly, up and down and round
and round, until the kitchen was trashed and
neither of them could harm the other, for they
were evenly matched. At last they stopped,
chests heaving, legs trembling, dripping with
sweat. Eee, it were as good as sex.

'I swear to God,' said Little John, 'you're
one of the best swordsmen I ever saw. If you

could shoot as well with a bow, you'd come to the greenwood with me and have two changes of clothing and 30 marks a year from Robin Hood.'

'Put up your sword,' said the cook. 'We're colleagues.' Then he brought Little John the numbles of a doe, with fine white bread and the best wine, and they ate and drank heartily; and when they had drunk well, they plighted their troth, so to speak, and swore they would be with Robin that very same night. They made their way to the treasure house as fast as they could, and even though the locks were of the strongest steel, they broke every one of them. They took the gold and silver vessels and everything they could get – gold pieces, drinking cups, silver spoons – they neglected nothing. They also took good solid money – £300 and more – and the cook took the best horse in the sheriff's stable, and they rode straight to Robin Hood in the ancient heart of the greenwood.

'God save you, dear Master!' cried Little John joyously. 'Christ save you and see you!'

'You are welcome,' said Robin Hood and embraced him warmly. 'And welcome also is this fair young fellow you bring with you. Now tell me, Little John, what news from Nottingham? We heard you'd become the sheriff's man and we were all trembling in our boots.'

'The proud sheriff greets you well,' said Little John, 'and sends you here by me, his cook, his silver vessels and £303 3s 3d 3 farthing.'

'By God's wallet,' said Robin, 'it was never by his good will that this bounty has come to me; it must be some sort of grant – enterprise allowance, perhaps.'

Little John was suddenly struck by the very devil of an idea, and he ran off into the forest. For five miles he ran, and everything happened as he willed it. For there he met the proud sheriff, hunting with hound and horn, and Little John, who could be courteous when he liked, knelt down before him. 'God save you, my love! Christ save you and see you!'

'Reynard Greenleaf!' said the sheriff. 'Where have you been all this time?'

'I've been in this forest all morning,' lied Little John, 'and a fair sight I have seen – in fact, it was the fairest sight I ever did see. Over yonder I saw a wondrous hart, his colour all green from the points of his antlers to the tips of his hooves, and a herd of seven score deer together with him and all green like him. But their antlers are so sharp, Master, of sixty of them or more, that I dare not shoot for dread that they would kill me.'

'By God's numbles!' swore the sheriff. 'That's a sight I'd like to see!'

'Then haste you thither, my darling, and straightaway come with me!'

The sheriff rode and Little John loped beside him like a great green greyhound, and when they came into the outlaws' camp, and seven score men in green had closed around the sheriff's little band of unhappy hunters, Little John pointed to Robin Hood and said with a grin, 'Lo, sir, here is the master hart I told you of.' The proud sheriff sat transfixed upon his horse.

'You sod, Greenleaf,' he muttered.

'I swear to God, darling,' said Little John, 'it's all your fault. I was misserved of my dinner when you left me at home.' Then they sat the sheriff down to supper and served him right royally on gleaming silver, and when the sheriff saw his own plate, he could not eat, he was so choked up.

'Cheer up, sheriff!' said Robin Hood. 'And because Little John is so fond of you, I will grant you your life.'

When they had supped and the day was all but gone, Robin told Little John to get his master ready for bed – take off his stockings and shoes, his tunic and his fine furred jacket, and give him a thin green cloak to wrap his body in. And Robin commanded his brave young men to lie in the same fashion under the greenwood tree, that the sheriff should see that was how they slept. And there was many a muttered curse and a '***k off!' but the sheriff was so wrapped up in his own misery, he scarcely noticed.

All that night the noble sheriff lay with just a thin green cloth twixt his naked body and the ground, and it was no wonder that, in the morning, when the sun rose and the birds began to sing, his whole body was stiff and bruised with aches and pains and he hadn't slept a wink.

'Cheer up, sheriff!' said Robin Hood. 'You'll get used to it. This is how our order sleeps under the greenwood tree.'

'Uuuuuuuh!' groaned the sheriff as he struggled to his feet. 'This is a harder order than a masochistic monk might devise. For all the gold in merry England I wouldn't live here any longer.'

'But sheriff,' said Robin, 'you shall dwell with me this whole twelvemonth. I'll teach you, proud sheriff, what it's like to be an outlaw.'

'Ooooooh Go-o-d!' groaned the sher-iff. 'Rather than stay here one more night, Robin, I beg you, strike off my head today and I will forgive you. But let me go, for sweet Mary the Mother, and I'll be the best friend you ever had.'

'Well,' said Robin, 'you shall swear on my bright sword by Mary the Mother of God that you will never seek to injure me by land or by water; and if you come across any of my men by night or by day, you will swear to help them if you may.'

> And now the sheriff has sworn his oath
> And home he has quickly gone
> And he is as full of the greenwood
> As a hip is full of stone.

The Fourth Fytte

The sheriff now dwelt in Nottingham and glad he was to be there, while Robin and his Merry Men walked by the woodland ways. And one day, well after noon: 'Robin, it's dinner time. Are we going to eat or not?' said Little John.

Robin said, 'No. For I fear that Our Lady is mad at me – she has not sent me my money.'

'Don't worry,' said Little John. 'The sun's not down yet and I dare swear the knight is honest.'

'Take your bow in hand,' said Robin. 'Let Much go with you and Will Scarlet too – and walk up to the Sayles on Watling Street again and wait there for some unknown guest; and whether he be a messenger or a minstrel, he shall have some good of me.'

Little John started out, half in annoyance at Robin's preprandial custom, girding himself with a good broadsword under his mantle of green. These three yeomen walked up to the Sayles plantation on Watling Street, where they looked east and west and saw no one; but when they looked back down the highway into Barnsdale, they saw two black monks, each sitting on a good palfrey. Then Little John said to Much, 'I'll lay my life on it – these monks have brought our pay; so lift up your hearts and your bows of yew and look that your hearts be steadfast, your bowstrings trusty and true. These monks have about fifty men with them and seven strong packhorses well loaded. They must be as rich as bishops. Now then, my brothers, we are only three but unless we bring them to dinner, we dare not look Robin in the face. So bend your bows and stop that crowd dead in its tracks. The foremost monk – his life and death are closed within my hand.' And when the dusty press of men and horses were well inside a good bow-shot, he notched an arrow to his string and bent his bow.

'Stay right there, you bastard monks!' cried Little John. 'And go no further. For if you do, by God, your death is in my hand and bad cess light on your heads, right under your hat-bands, for making our master wait for his dinner.'

'Who is your master?' yelled the monk.

'Robin Hood,' said Little John.

'That filthy footpad!' snarled the monk. 'I never heard any good of him!'

'You lie!' cried Little John. 'He is an honest yeoman and he bids you dine with him.'

'Never!' cried the monk and began to raise his arm, but John let loose his arrow and it whistled through the deadly air and thudded home into the monk's breast; he toppled from his horse onto the ground and lay still. At the same time, Much and Scarlet sent their arrows into the hearts of the two officers of the convoy; and after a bit of milling about in sheer panic, and six other men bleeding their lives out into the dust of the road, the rest fled, leaving the other fat monk quivering with terror and the seven packhorses wild-eyed at the smell of blood. The outlaws led the monk and the pack-horses to the door of Robin's lodge. Robin doffed his hood when he went to greet the monk, but the monk was not so courteous and left his on.

'By dear worthy God,' sighed Little John, 'he's a complete churl and no mistake.'

'No matter,' said Robin. 'He knows no courtesy. How many men did this monk have, John?'

'Fifty-two when we met,' said John, 'but some of them have gone away now – for good.'

'Blow a horn!' cried Robin, 'that we may be in fellowship.' And seven score brave yeomen were soon gathered in the clearing, each one of them with a fine cloak of striped scarlet. They made the monk wash and wipe himself before they sat him down to dinner, and Robin Hood and Little John served him themselves.

'Dig in, monk,' said Robin.

'Er – g-grammercy, s-sir,' he stammered.

'Where is your abbey, monk, when you're at home? And who is your patron saint?'

'Er – St Mary's Abbey,' said the monk, though I hold but humble office there.'

'What office?' said Robin.

'Um – er – sir, the high cellarer.'

'You are the more welcome,' said Robin, 'so might I thrive! Fill his cup with the best wine, for this monk will drink to me. But monk – I have been marvelling greatly all day long. I fear that Our Lady is cross with me, for she has not sent me my money.'

'Oh, have no doubt, Master,' said Little John. 'There's no need to worry. This monk has surely brought it, I dare well swear, for he belongs to her abbey.'

'She was a guarantor,' said Robin, 'for a certain knight, for a little money I lent him, right here under this tree. And if you have indeed brought me that silver, I pray you let me have a look at it; and I shall give you a helping hand, whenever you have need of one.'

The monk then swore a vile oath, with a long face: 'By St Mary's loins, I never heard of this guarantee you're talking about.'

'By God's stones!' said Robin. 'Monk, you're mad! For God is held to be a righteous man and so is his mum. You told me with your own tongue – you can't deny it – that you are her servant and serve her every day, and now she has made you her messenger, to pay me my money; so I am grateful that you have come on the very day. What's in your coffers? Tell me the truth now!'

'S-s-sir,' he said, 'only 20 marks, so may I prosper!'

'If there's no more,' said Robin, 'I'll not take a penny. And if you have need of more, good sir, I'll lend it you. But if I find more, I reckon you shall forgo it – but of your spending money, monk, I'll not take any. Go now, Little John, and tell me the truth – if there's no more than 20 marks, I'll not touch a penny of it.'

Little John spread his cloak down, as he had done before, and he counted out of the monk's trunks £800 and more. Little John let it lie there, nice and still, and went quickly to his master, saying, 'Sir Richard was right – Our Lady has doubled your outlay.'

'I swear to God!' said Robin. 'Monk, what did I tell you? Our Lady is the truest woman I've ever come across. By God's loan agreement, I could search through the whole of England and never find a better guarantor for my money. Fill his cup with the best wine and make him drink, and greet well your gracious Lady from me, monk, and if she ever have need of Robin Hood, she'll find a friend in me. And if she needs any more silver, then come to me again and, by this token she has sent me, she shall have three times as much.'

This monk had been going down to London, to a great meeting being held by the abbot, the Lord High Justice, the Sheriff of Nottingham and several other powerful Normans, to try to bring the knight that now rode so high under their foot – but he did not tell Robin that, for when Robin said, 'Whither are you riding, monk?' he replied, 'Sir, to certain manors in this part of the country, to reckon with our reeves and stewards, who have done much wrong and are cheating us.'

'Come here, Little John,' said Robin. 'I know no better yeoman for searching a monk's trunk. We've got all the loot from the packhorses. See if there's anything on the other monk's horse.'

'By Our Lady!' swore the monk. 'That is no courtesy, to bid a man to dinner and then beat and bind and rob him blind!'

'It is our ancient custom,' said Robin. 'But go your ways, monk. We'll not take your spending money and you can take the other horse back to St Mary.'

The monk mounted up on his horse – no longer was he inclined to stay.

'Have another drink,' said Robin, 'one for t' road.'

'No, by God!' said the monk. 'I'm sorry I came so near. I'd've dined more cheaply in Blyth or Doncaster.'

'Greet your abbot well,' said Robin, 'and also your prior, I pray you. And bid them send me such a monk to dinner every day.'

◁

And now we will leave this monk alone and talk once more of Sir Richard Attlee, for he came to keep his day while it was still light. From Wentbridge he rode straight into Barnsdale Forest, deep within the greenwood, and there he found Robin Hood and all his

Merry Men. Sir Richard slipped lightly down from his horse, courteously doffed his hood and went down on one knee, saying, 'God save you, Robin Hood, and all this brave company!'

'You are welcome, gentle knight,' said Robin, 'but what great need has driven you to the greenwood now? I pray you tell me, Sir Richard – why have you been so long away from me?'

'Because the abbot of St Mary's and the Lord High Justice were still trying to get my land,' said the knight, 'and it was all I could do to stop them.'

'And have you your land again?' said Robin. 'Is it secure now? Tell me the truth.'

'Yes, by the love of God,' said the knight, 'and for that I thank both God and you – but don't take it amiss that I have been so long getting here today. I came past a wrestling match at Wentbridge and there I helped a poor yeoman who was being sorely wronged. In fact, when he heard I was coming here, he asked to come with me. I think you've got a new outlaw, Robin. Meet Gilbert of the White Hand.' And the young wrestler stepped forward and Robin shook his very white hand.

'Nay, for God's sake, Sir Richard,' said Robin, 'for that I thank you heartily. Anyone who helps out an honest yeoman will be my friend for life.' Then Sir Richard said, 'And I am here, Robin, to pay you back the £400 which you lent me a year ago; and here also are 20 marks for your courtesy to me.'

'No, no, for heaven's sake,' said Robin. 'Keep your money and enjoy the use of it forever; for Our Lady has sent me my money by her high cellarer and if I took it twice, then shame on me.' And Robin told the knight the story of the monk, and they laughed loud and long together.

'But I must keep my word,' insisted the knight. 'Your money is right here in my coffers.'

'Use it well,' said Robin, 'for I know you are a gentle and a generous knight, and welcome you are here, under my trysting tree – but what are all these bows and these fine feathered arrows?'

'In God's truth,' said the knight, 'they are but a poor present to you from me.'

'Come here, Little John,' said Robin. 'Go to the treasury and bring us the £400 extra that the monk paid us. And you shall have that £400, O true and gentle knight, and buy yourself horses and fine harnesses and gilded spurs; and if ever you lack spending money, come to Robin Hood and you'll be in want no longer; and use well this £400 I got from Our Lady in York and take my advice – let not your affairs get so threadbare again.'

> Thus good Robyn helped the knight
> Out of all his trouble and care
> And God that sits in heaven on high
> Grant us as well to fare.

The Fifth Fytte

Now the knight had taken his leave and gone upon his way, Robin Hood and his Merry Men lived quietly for many a day.

Now attend and listen, gentle folk, and hear what I shall say: how the proud Sheriff of Nottingham proclaimed a great contest – that all the best archers of the north should come on a certain day, and they that shot the best of all should win the game; and he that shot the furthest both fair and low, at a pair of fine targets set up under the fringes of the greenwood, should win a wonderful arrow, the shaft of pure white silver, the head and feathers of rich red-gold – there was no other like it in the whole of merry England.

Robin heard about this under his trysting tree and said, 'Make you ready, my strong young men, I'd like to see this shooting match, so get your gear together, my merry young men, and I will test the sheriff's faith, to see if his word is true.'

When they had shouldered their bows and slung their quivers of brightly feathered arrows on their backs, seven score strong young men stood at Robin's knee; and when they got to Nottingham, they saw that the butts were a goodly length and set up just within the edges of the forest, no doubt to allay their fears, and there was many a bold archer there that shot with a good strong bow.

'Only six will shoot with me,' said Robin. 'The others will stand by with their good bows bent in case of betrayal.' The fourth outlaw to bend his bow was Robin Hood, and the sheriff was well aware of that as he stood by the butts. Three times Robin shot in turn and he always slit the wand, and so did good Gilbert of the White Hand. Little John and Will Scarlet were also good archers, and so was little Much the Miller's Son; and in Little John the furious sheriff recognised his former servant, Reynold Greenleaf. These four were all better than anyone else; but when they had shot in turn, evermore the best of them, in truth, was Robin Hood; so the silver arrow was awarded to him, for he was the worthiest, and he took the prize courteously and modestly. He then would have gone back into the greenwood – but there was a great cry of 'Robin Hood! It's Robin Hood!' and great horns began to blow.

'Woe are you worth! Treason!' cried Robin. 'Full evil are you to know! And woe are you, proud sheriff, treating your guest like this! You promised me otherwise in the wild forest yonder; but if I had you again in the greenwood, under my trysting tree, you should give me a better pledge than your lying word!' (Thus we see that there are always liars in public places and you can never trust the people in power.)

Then many a bow was bent and many an arrow hissed through the deadly air, many a shirt was rent and many a side was pierced. The outlaws' shooting was so fast and furious that no man could stand up to them, and the sheriff's men fled away as quickly as they could. Robin saw that the ambush was broken, and would have been back in the greenwood as swiftly as he might, but still the arrows flew thick and fast and Little John was wounded badly, with an arrow right through his knee, so that he could neither walk nor ride – it was a great blow.

'Master!' gasped Little John. 'If ever you loved me, and for that same Lord's love that died upon a tree, and as a reward for all my services to you, never let the sheriff find me alive – but take out your bright sword and cut off my head and give me wounds so deep and wide that no life be left in me.'

'I wouldn't do that,' said Robin. 'John, I would not have you slain for all the gold in merry England, though it lay here now upon the ground.'

'God forbid,' said Much, 'that you, Little John, should now part company with us.' And he took him up on his back and bore him for well over a mile, though many a time he laid him down and shot for a while, for still the sheriff's men pursued them, shooting at them the whole time, reinforced now by more soldiers from Nottingham.

Then they saw a fair castle a little way within the wood – a double ditch lay all around it and a good high wall, by the Holy Cross; and there now lived that gentle knight, Sir Richard Attlee, to whom Robin had lent money in the forest. He took Robin and all his company in, saying, 'Welcome are you, good Robin Hood, welcome are you to me – I thank you heartily for all the comfort you gave me and for your courtesy, and for all your great kindness to me under the greenwood tree. I love no man in all the world as much as you and for all that the proud Sheriff of Nottingham can do, you'll be all right in here; so shut the gates and draw up the drawbridge and let no man come in, and arm yourselves well, my men, and make you ready and get up onto the walls – for one thing I ask of you, Robin, by St Quentin, is that you stay with me now for forty days, feasting and eating and making merry.' So tables were laid and beds were made and fresh clothes were laid out, swiftly and efficiently, and Robin Hood and his Merry Men sat down to their dinner.

The Sixth Fytte

Now listen up, you gentle folk, and hearken to your ballad what I'm singing for you: listen how the proud Sheriff of Nottingham and an army of men-at-arms came quickly to stir up the countryside and to besiege the walls of the knight's castle all around; and there the proud sheriff cried loudly, 'You traitor knight! You are holding the king's enemies here against the law!'

'Sir!' called Sir Richard from the battlements, 'I will justify my actions and all the deeds that have been done here, or forfeit all my lands, as I am a true knight. Wend forth, sirs, upon your way and trouble me no more, until you know the will of the king and hear what he will say to you.'

So the sheriff had his answer and no mistake, and forth he rode to London town to tell all unto the king. There he told tales to the king about the knight and about Robin Hood, and also about the bold archers that were so noble and good.

'The false knight will avow what he has done,' whinged the sheriff, 'in keeping these violent outlaws safe in his castle. He will be lord of the whole North Country and set you at nought.'

'I will be at Nottingham,' said our king, 'within this fortnight, and I will take Robin Hood and I will take that knight. Go home now, sheriff; do as I tell you and equip yourself with enough good archers from the countryside around.'

So the sheriff took his leave and went on his way, and on a certain day Robin Hood went back to the greenwood. And some time later Little John was healed of the arrow that had shot him in the knee and went straight back to Robin Hood under his trysting tree.

So Robin walked once again in the forest under the leaves so green and that gave the proud Sheriff of Nottingham a great deal of vexation, for the sheriff missed out there on Robin Hood – he might not have his prey. So he stalked the gentle knight both by night and day. Ever he lay in wait for this gentle knight, Sir Richard Attlee, as he went hawking down by the riverside, where he let his hawks fly free. And there he took this gentle knight with a small army of heavily armed men and led him towards Nottingham, bound hand and foot; and as they rode along through the forest the sheriff swore a great oath. 'By Him that died on tree, I'd rather have Robin Hood than this man or £100.'

Now the knight's wife heard this, for she had escaped the posse's notice and was hiding hard by in a thicket. She was a fair lady and a free one, and she spurred on her good palfrey to gallop deeper into the greenwood; and when she came to Robin's trysting tree deep in the heart of the forest, she found there Robin Hood and all his fair company.

'God save thee, good Robin,' she cried, 'and all thy company; and for Our Dear Lady's sake, I pray you, grant me a boon! Never let my wedded lord be shamefully slain; for he is fast bound and brought towards Nottingham, all for love of thee.'

Robin said to that lady so free, 'What man has taken your lord?'

'The proud Sheriff of Nottingham,' she said. 'I tell you the truth, Robin; they are not yet three miles upon the way.' Robin started up, like a man that has gone mad.

'Hurry, my Merry Men, for Him that died on the cross!' he cried. 'And he that forsakes this sorry business shall no longer dwell in the greenwood with me.'

Soon there were some good bows bent, more than seven score – and they spared neither hedge nor ditch that stood before them.

'I swear to God!' gasped Robin. 'I would fain see the sheriff and if I may take him, I'll even the score.' And when they came to Nottingham, they ran through the streets and soon they met up with the Sheriff.

'Wait, proud sheriff!' cried Robin. 'Stay and speak with me! I would dearly love to hear some tidings of our comely king. I've not gone so fast on foot for seven year, by God, and I swear to God, proud sheriff, it's not for the sake of your health!'

Robin then bent a full good bow, and with all his will he drove an arrow into the sheriff so hard that he slammed into the ground and lay there very still; and even so, before he could arise again and stand upon his feet, Robin hacked off the sheriff's head with his bright sword.

'Lie there, proud sheriff!' he said. 'And may the devil take your soul! No man could trust you while you were alive!' His men drew out their own bright swords, so sharp and keen, and laid into the sheriff's men and mowed them down before them. Robin went over to the knight, where he lay bound across his own horse, and cut his bonds in two. He put a bow in his hand and bade him stand.

'Leave your horse behind,' said Robin, 'and learn how to run. You shall come with me to the greenwood, through mire, moss and fen. You shall come with me to the greenwood without more ado, until I can win for us both the grace of Edward, our comely king.'

The Seventh Fytte

The king himself then came to Nottingham with a great array of knights, to take that gentle knight Sir Richard Attlee, and also Robin Hood, if he could. He enquired among the men of that district about Robin Hood and about that gentle knight, who was so bold and steadfast. And when they had told him the whole case, our king understood their tale and seized all the knight's lands into his own hand. Then he travelled both near and far throughout the North Country, even as far as the pass of Lancashire, until he came back round to Plumpton Park near Knaresborough in the West Riding, and there he missed many of his deer. There, where he was used to seeing many a fine fat hart, he could hardly find one single deer with a good set of horns. The king was full of wondrous wrath at this and swore by the Trinity: 'I would I had Robin Hood where I could see him with my own two eyes! He that would smite off the knight's head and bring it to me shall have all the lands of Sir Richard at the bloody Lea! I give them to him with my charter and seal it with my own hand, to have and to hold for evermore in merry England.'

Then up spoke a good old knight, a local man, that was true of speech and straight of talk: 'Eee, my liege lord the king, I'll just say a word to thee. There's no man in the North Country can keep Sir Richard's lands, while Robin Hood rides or runs and bears a bow in's hands – for that man would lose his head and a man's head is the best ball in his hood; so don't give the knight's lands to any man, my lord king, you mean to do good to.'

Half a year and more dwelt our comely king in Nottingham, and in all that time he heard no news of Robin Hood, not even what county he was in. But always good Robin went by hiding place and hill, and always he slew the king's deer and ate of them his fill.

Then up spoke a good old forester that stood by the king's knee: 'If you want to see Robin, you must do as I do. Take five of the best knights in your company and walk down to yonder abbey and get yourselves monks' gear. I'll be your guide and lead you on your way and before you get back to Nottingham, I'll lay my head on it, you'll meet up with Robin, if he be still alive; ere you reach Nottingham again, you'll see him with your own two eyes.'

Very quickly our king was kitted out and so were his five knights, every one of them in monkish garb, and most merrily they came away. Our king was a big burly bloke with a broad hat on his crown so he looked right abbot-like as they rode back up to town. Stiff boots our king had on as well and he rode singing to the greenwood, his fellow

monks all clothed in grey. Heavily laden
packhorses followed on behind our king,
until they came into the greenwood, a mile
under the trees. And there they met with
Robin Hood, standing on the track, and so
did many a bold archer, I can tell you. Robin
quickly caught hold of the king's horse and
said, 'Sir abbot, by your leave, you must
stay with us a while. We are yeomen of this
forest, living under the greenwood tree, and
we live by killing the king's deer – we have
no other shift by which to live. But you have
churches and rents and plenty of gold, so
give us some of your spending money, for
the charity of the saints.'

Then up spoke our comely king: 'I have
brought no more than £40 into the
greenwood with me; for I have been in
Nottingham with the king this past fortnight
and there I've spent a great deal of money on
many a great lord and many a fine banquet;
and so I've only £40 left. But if I had £100
I would vouchsafe it thee.' Robin took the

£40 and divided it in two. Half he gave to his Merry Men and bade them get merry on it. Then Robin said courteously, 'Sir, have this other half for spending and have a nice day – we shall meet again, I feel sure of it.'

'Grammercy!' said the king. 'But Edward our king greets you well and sends you his seal, and bids you come to Nottingham to feast right royally with him.' He took out the king's great seal so they could all see it and Robin knew his manners and went down on one knee.

'I love no man in all the world as well as I do my king. Welcome is my lord's seal and welcome are you, monk, for your tidings – and for these tidings, sir abbot, you shall dine with me today, here under my trysting tree, for the love of my king.'

Then forth he led our comely king, most gently by the hand; and many a deer was slain there and swiftly prepared for the feast. Robin raised a great hunting horn and blew a loud blast, and seven score strong young men came running up in right good order and knelt down full fairly before Robin; and the king said to himself and swore by St Augustine, 'Here is a wondrous, well-ordered sight, by God's pain; his men are more swiftly at his bidding than my men are at mine.'

Their dinner was quickly got ready and they sat down to it and both Robin and Little John served our king as well as they could. And soon before the king was set a dish of the best venison, with fine white bread, good red wine, and light and brown ale too.

'Make good cheer, Sir Abbot,' said Robin, 'for the love of charity and for your tidings from the king, may you be blessed for evermore. Now you shall see what kind of life we lead before you go on your way and then you can inform the king when you see him next.'

Straightaway all the outlaws leapt to their feet, their bows smartly bent. The king was never so frightened in his life – he was sure they were going to shoot him. But two rods were set up and to them they made their way, and the king reckoned the marks were too long by fifty paces. Around the tip of each rod was woven a rose garland, at which they shot.

'Whoever misses the garland,' said Robin, 'shall forfeit his hunting tackle and yield it to his better, be it never so fine; for I will spare no man, so may I drink ale or wine. And he will bear a buffet to his head – with the hood down, mind!' And when anyone had the misfortune to be drawn with Robin, he smote them wondrous hard.

Two full rounds did Robin shoot and he always split the wand, and so did Gilbert of the White Hand. Little John and Will Scarlet spared nothing in their attempts to win but, when they missed the garland, Robin gave them both a hefty wallop. But at the last shot, in spite of how his friends had fared, Robin missed the garland by three fingers and more.

Then up spoke Gilbert. 'Master,' he said, 'your tackle is forfeit to me. Now stand up here and take your pay.'

'If it be so,' said Robin, 'there's nothing for it – but I pray you, sir abbot, I will deliver my arrow to you and you must give me my pay.'

'By your leave, Robin,' said the king, 'it is against the rules of my order to hit a good yeoman, in case I should give him grief.'

'Buffet me boldly,' said Robin. 'I give you all the leave you want – and absolution as well.' (He was thinking that a man of God would be gentler than a brawny outlaw.) With that, the king folded up his sleeve and gave Robin such a buffet that he knocked him sprawling on the ground.

'I swear to God!' cried Robin. 'You're a hunk of a monk! There's pith in your arm and I'll bet you can shoot as well.' And thus did our king and Robin Hood begin to meet with each other; for, with the blow, the king's hood had fallen from his head and Robin beheld our handsome king and looked him intently in the face; and so did Sir Richard Attlee, and they both knelt down. And so did all those wild outlaws, when they saw them kneel.

'My lord king of England,' said Robin, 'now I know you well.'

'Mercy then, Robin,' said the king, 'under your trysting tree – of your goodness and your grace – mercy for my men and me.'

'Yes, for God,' said Robin. 'And God save me, I ask mercy, my lord king, for my men and me.'

'Yes, for God,' said the king. 'It is for that I have come, provided you leave the greenwood with all your company and come home, sir, to my court and live with me there.'

'I swear to God,' said Robin, 'right so shall it be. I will come to your court to see what service with you is like and bring seven score and three of my men with me; but if your service doesn't agree with me, I will return again full soon and shoot at the brown deer as I am wont to do.'

The Eighth Fytte

'Have you any green cloth,' said the king,
'that you'll now sell to me?'

'Yes, by God,' said Robin, 'three and
thirty yards.'

'Robin,' said the king, 'now, I pray you,
sell some of that cloth to me and my men.'

'Yes, by God,' said Robin, 'or else I were
a fool. I know that on another day you will
clothe me in your own livery at Christmas.'

The king cast off his cowl and put on a
green garment, and soon every knight had
one on as well. When they were all clothed
in Lincoln green, they cast away their grey
habits and the king said gaily, 'Now we shall
to Nottingham!' Their bows bent, away they
went, shooting all together in company, all
outlaws together, towards Nottingham town.
Our king and Robin rode side by side, I tell
you not a lie, and played at pluck-buffet as
they went on their way; and our king won
many a buffet from Robin Hood that day

and good Robin did not spare the king at all in the payment of his pay.

'God help me!' cried the king. 'There's no learning the games you play – I couldn't beat you at shooting though I shot the whole year through.'

All the people of Nottingham just stood and stared – they saw nothing but green mantles covering the entire field. Then each man said to another, 'I fear our king is slain! And if Robin Hood gets into the town, he'll not leave one of us alive.' Very quickly then they began to run – yeomen and knaves, and old wives that could barely hobble along hopped upon their crutches.

The king laughed loud and long and commanded them to come back; and when they saw our comely king, I'll bet they were relieved. They ate and drank and made merry there in Nottingham town, with much minstrelsy and gladsome singing. Then up spoke our noble king to Sir Richard Attlee: 'I give you here your lands

again and in future try to be a good man.'
Robin went down on one knee and said,
'I thank you, my noble king, for your goodness to my friend Sir Richard, and I swear to
serve you truly all the days of my life.'

But Robin had dwelt at the king's court
in London town for only a year and three
months, and in that time he had spent more
than £100 and all his men's wages; for every
post at court that Robin held, he had to lay
down more and more money, to knights and
squires and suchlike, to win renown and
power and a higher place in the pecking order.
By the time the year was all but gone, he
had only two men left – Little John and Will
Scarlet – all the rest had gone home in disgust.

One fine day Robin saw some young men
shooting. 'Alas!' said Robin. 'My wealth is
all gone. At one time I was a good archer,
stiff and strong; in fact, I was accounted the
best archer in the whole of merry England.
Alas and well away! If I dwell any longer
here with the king, sorrow itself will slay me.'

So Robin Hood went to the king and said, 'My lord king of England, grant me what I ask. I built a chapel in Barnsdale – a pretty place dedicated to Mary Magdalene – and it is there I want to be. For these past seven nights I haven't slept a wink, neither for these past seven days have I had aught to eat or drink. I long with all my heart to go to Barnsdale. I may no longer stay away – barefoot and clad in wool I have sworn to go.'

'If it be so,' said King Edward, 'there's nothing for it. For seven nights and no longer I give you leave to dwell away from me.'

'Grammercy, My Lord,' said Robin and went down on his knee, then took his leave most courteously and went to the greenwood.

When he came to the greenwood on a merry morning, he heard the merry notes of the small birds singing. 'It's a long time,' said Robin, 'since I was last here. I rather think it would do me good to shoot the king's deer.' When Robin had shot a great red hart, he blew his horn. All the outlaws of the forest knew that horn-call well and gathered together in a short space of time – seven score strong young men came running up in right good order and gaily doffed their hoods and went down on one knee.

'Welcome!' they cried. 'Dear Master, under this greenwood tree!'

And Robin dwelt in the greenwood for twenty-two more years and, for fear of Edward our noble king, he never left the forest again. Yet he was beguiled, I know, by a wicked woman, the Prioress of Kirklees, who was a close kinswoman of his – all for her love of a knight, Sir Roger of Doncaster, who was her own special lover, devil take them both! They took counsel together to decide how they might best slay Robin Hood.

Up spoke Robin in his camp under the greenwood tree: 'Tomorrow I must go to Kirklees to be bled skilfully by my cousin the

Prioress.' Sir Roger of Doncaster lay by the Prioress in her bed, and there they betrayed good Robin Hood through their false and deceitful games. Christ that died on the cross have mercy on his soul! For he was a good outlaw and did poor men much good.

Six

The Play of 'Robin Hood and the Friar'

All sing: How many merry months be in the
            year?
            There are thirteen, I say,
            And the midsummer moon is the mer-
            riest of all,
            Next to the merry month of May.

Here begins the Play of Robin Hood, very
proper to be played in May Games.

Actors: Robin Hood, Little John, Maid
Marian, Friar Tuck and his Two Dogs:
Cut and Bause.

Robin Hood:	Now stand you forth, my merry men all
	And hear what I shall say;
	Of an adventure I shall tell you,
	The which befell the other day.
	As I went by the highway,
	With a stout friar I met,
	A quarter staff in his hand,
	And lightly to me he leapt,
	And still he bade me stand.
	There were strokes two or three,
	But I cannot tell who had the worse;
	But well I know the whoreson leapt within me,
	And from me took my purse.
	Now is there any of my Merry Men all

That to that friar will go,
And bring him forth to me withall,
Whether he will or no?

Little   Yes, Master, I swear to God,
John: To that friar I will go
             And bring him forth to you withall,
             Whether he will or no.

Friar Tuck: (who enters after the others depart)
             Deus hic! Deus hic! God be here!
             Is not this a holy word for a friar?
             God save all this company!
             But am I not a jolly friar?
             For I can shoot both far and near
             And handle the sword and buckler
             And this quarter staff also.
             If I meet with a gentleman or a yeoman,
             I am not afraid to look upon him,
             Nor boldly with him to carpe;
             And if he speaks any words to me,
             He shall have strokes two or three,
             That shall make his body smart.

But, masters, to show you the matter,
Wherefore and why I am come hither,
In faith I will not spare.
I am come to seek a good yeoman,
In Barnsdale men say is his habitation:
And his name is Robin Hood,
And if that he be a better man than I,
His servant will I be and serve him truly;
But if that I be a better man than he,
By my truth my knave shall he be,
And lead these dogs all three.
[Actually, there are only two.]

Robin: (entering and grasping the friar round
         the throat)
         Yield, friar, in your long coat!

Tuck: I beshrew your heart, knave, you're
         hurting my throat!

Robin: I believe, friar, you're beginning to dote:
         Who made you so malapert and bold
         To come into this forest here
         Among my fallow deer?

Tuck: Go de-louse yourself, ragged knave!
If you make many words, I'll give you one on the ear,
Though I be but a poor friar.
To seek Robin Hood I am come here
And to him my heart to break.

Robin: You lousy friar, what would you with him?
He never loved friar nor none of friars' kin.

Tuck: Avaunt, you ragged knave!
Or you shall have it on the skin.

Robin: Of all the men to meet in the morning, you are the worst!
To meet with you I have no lust.
For he that meets with a fox or a friar in the morning,
To speed ill that day he stands in jeopardy;
Therefore I had rather meet with the

devil in hell,
Friar, I tell you as I think,
Than meet with a friar or a fox
In the morning, before I drink.

Tuck: Avaunt, you ragged knave, this is but
a mock!
If you make many more words, you
shall have a knock.

Robin: Hark, friar, to what I say here;
Over this water you shall me bear,
For the bridge is born away.

Tuck: To say you nay I will not;
To let you off your oath, it were a
great pity and a sin;
So up on a friar's back and have with
you even in.

Robin: (climbing up on the friar's back)
Nay, friar, have over.

Tuck: Now am I, friar, within and you,
            Robin, without,
            But to lay you here I have no great doubt
            (throwing Robin into the river)
            Now are you, Robin, within and I,
            friar, without,
            So lie there, knave, and choose
            whether you will sink or swim.

Robin: Why, you lousy friar, what have you
            done?!

Tuck: Marry, set a knave over his shoes.

Robin: I'll get you for this!

Tuck: Why, will you fight a pluck? [a bout]
Robin: And God send me good luck.

Tuck: Then have a stroke from Friar Tuck.

(They fight and Robin gets the worst of it.)

Robin: Hold your hand, friar, and hear me
          speak!

Tuck: Say on, ragged knave,
          It seems to me you begin to sweat.

Robin: In this forest I have a hound;
          I would not sell him for a hundred
          pound.
          Give me leave my horn to blow
          So that my faithful hound may know.

Tuck: Blow on, ragged knave, without any
          doubt,
          Blow till both your eyes start out.

(Robin blows his horn. Enter Little John and
Maid Marian, a man in drag.)

          Here be a sort of ragged knaves
          come in,
          All clothed in Kendal green,
          And to you they take their way now.

Robin: 'Appen they do.

Tuck: I gave you leave to blow at your will;
        Now give me leave to whistle my fill.

Robin: Whistle, friar, evilly might you fare!
        Whistle until both your eyes start to stare!

(Enter two men in dog costumes)

Tuck: Now Cut and Bause!
        Bring forth the clubs and staves,
        And have down with these ragged
        knaves.

(They fight, or rather, perform a Morris
stick dance)

Robin: How say you, friar, will you be my man,
        To do me the best service you can?
        You shall have both gold and fee
        And also here is a lady free (he offers
        him Maid Marian)

I will give her unto thee
And her chaplain I thee make
To serve her for my sake.

Tuck: Here is a handsome hussy,
A yard up to her pussy.
She is a trollop, I trust,
To serve a friar's lust,
A pricker, a prancer, a tearer of sheets,
A wagger of bollocks while men lie
asleep.
Go home, you knaves, flick your crabs
in the fire
For my lady and I will dance in the
mire for very pure joy!